Teaching Signature Thinking

T0386583

How do you help students uncover and hone their innate talents to create works that are uniquely their own, works worthy of their signatures? This unique new book guides teachers with practical, research-based strategies that can be used to make creativity the new normal in classrooms.

You'll learn how to equip students with the knowledge necessary to innovate in a field, and how to help students embrace a risk-ready environment. You'll also find out how to help students tinker and build prototypes through project-based learning.

With the step-by-step guidance in this book, students will be able to bring their creativity to life and will be more prepared to leave their mark on the world.

John Lando Carter is an assistant professor of education at Middle Tennessee State University and a former secondary ELA and creative writing teacher. He teaches classes in the *Assessment, Learning, and Student Success Ed.D. Program* at MTSU.

Kevin S. Krahenbuhl, Ed.D., is Associate Professor of Education and Program Director for the *Assessment, Learning, and Student Success Ed.D. Program* at Middle Tennessee State University. He has spent his entire professional life in public schools and is committed to working with public schools to improve learning for all students. He is also author of *Building Effective Learning Environments* (Routledge, 2020) and *The Decay of Truth in Education* (Cambridge Scholars, 2018).

Teaching Signature Thinking

Strategies for Unleashing
Creativity in the Classroom

John Lando Carter & Kevin S. Krahenbuhl

Routledge
Taylor & Francis Group

NEW YORK AND LONDON

Cover image: © Getty Images

First published 2022
by Routledge
605 Third Avenue, New York, NY 10158

and by Routledge
4 Park Square, Milton Park, Abingdon, Oxon, OX14 4RN

Routledge is an imprint of the Taylor & Francis Group, an informa business

Library of Congress Cataloging-in-Publication Data
A catalog record for this title has been requested

ISBN: 978-1-032-06250-1 (hbk)
ISBN: 978-1-032-04545-0 (pbk)
ISBN: 978-1-003-20138-0 (ebk)

DOI: 10.4324/9781003201380

Typeset in Palatino
by codeMantra

Contents

Authors

John Lando Carter is an assistant professor of education at Middle Tennessee State University and a former secondary ELA and creative writing teacher. He teaches classes in the *Assessment, Learning, and Student Success Ed.D. Program* at MTSU.

Kevin S. Krahenbuhl, Ed.D., is Associate Professor of Education and Program Director for the *Assessment, Learning, and Student Success Ed.D. Program* at Middle Tennessee State University. He has spent his entire professional life in public schools and is committed to working with public schools to improve learning for all students. He is also author of *Building Effective Learning Environments* (Routledge, 2020) and *The Decay of Truth in Education* (Cambridge Scholars, 2018).

lecture on how bad lecturing is for learning? He also questioned why he was spending money to learn from experts with no K-12 experience who often left the learning up to students with no knowledge of the craft. The students didn't know where they were going or what their purpose was; they didn't have a clue. So Kevin struggled for years to strike a balance for his own students between *understanding accurately* and *being curious*. However, it all came together when he and Lando had the great privilege of butting heads. Lando is the resident dreamer. Kevin is the resident skeptic. This tension of opposites is what makes the team work. It is also central to how the fusion of our experiences and expertise led us to the framework we are excited to share with you: *Signature Thinking*.

1

Getting Started with Signature Thinking: So What Is Signature Thinking?

Have you ever had a student turn in a project that stops you in your tracks? The student gave you everything you asked for *and* something a little bit different? Us too. We pause and wonder: how did they do that? Instead of students surprising us with creative works, we want creativity to happen by design. We want students to uncover and hone their innate talents to create works that are uniquely their own, works worthy of their signatures. Think about the signature works of visionaries. The Sistine Chapel. The Apple iPhone. How quickly do we know it's a Prince song or a Frank Lloyd Wright design? Immediately. Their creations are striking in nature and one of a kind. We want students to develop their own signatures too.

Signature Thinking guides teachers with practical, research-based strategies that can be used to make creativity the new normal in classrooms. We begin with intentionally designing curriculum to cultivate creativity. Next, we equip students with the knowledge necessary to be creative in a field. With that knowledge in place, we teach students to embrace a *risk-ready environment* where they actively take risks and challenge the very

DOI: 10.4324/9781003201380-1

knowledge acquired through talking in what ifs and maybes. They are then ready to tinker and build prototypes through the power of project-based learning and become *signature thinkers.*

So What Is Creativity Anyway?

During our creativity workshops we love to start with a word association game. We place the words "Creativity is…" on the screen and have teachers brainstorm the words that flood their minds. Here are some of the words that come up again and again:

◆ Messy	◆ Rebellious	◆ Passion
◆ Non-linear	◆ Engaging	◆ Challenging
◆ Cyclical	◆ Empowering	◆ Joyful
◆ Risky	◆ Groundbreaking	◆ Fun

These words are incredible! Don't you wish for students to feel these sensations while in school? These are precisely the words that define the feeling of being creative. However, there is a research definition of creativity that is important to know. The image below (Figure 1.1) synthesizes the work from renowned creativity researchers over the last 50 or so years.

In short, creativity means that the ideas are novel and original but also useful, meaning they really work *and* work inside the context or domain at hand (medicine, English class, etc.). Ronald Beghetto, a leading creativity expert, cautions that "aimless

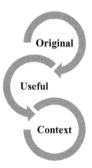

FIGURE 1.1

exploration and unconstrained originality are not creativity. Creativity requires opportunities for original expression in a meaningful context, which includes task constraints and criteria for success."[1] So, it is our task as teachers and mentors to help our students not only generate original ideas but also shape them into working innovations that successfully challenge the status quo. Let's recap: creativity means producing something original, but it has to work, and it has to work in the right context.

There are two final creativity definitions that are crucial to understand before moving forward: *Big-C* and *little-c* creativity.[2] We will tell a story to define each term and set the stage for what we aim to accomplish with *Signature Thinking*.

Jonas Salk, one of the most prolific scientific minds of the 20th century, was known even as a second-year medical student to challenge his professors with pesky questions and impossible ideas. Upon presenting the basic germ of what would become his signature polio vaccine to his professor, he received a simple *no*. When Salk pressed for an explanation, he received a simple *because*. Experts sometimes can narrow their view through too much knowledge, causing a sense of creative tunnel vision. The expert, in this case, could not see the apprentice's vision. But the most creative people in history have always been able to oscillate from *what is* to *what could be* in order to tilt the world from the *inconceivable* to the *conceivable*. Salk continued poking and prodding at the edges of his domain; he kept asking *what if* and searching for hidden patterns. A few years later, Salk proved that we could indeed use ultraviolet light to neutralize a virus and leverage that process to save countless children from the horrors of polio. As Csikszentmihalyi recounts beautifully in his book *Creativity*, the "widespread use of what came to be called the Salk vaccine almost completely eradicated an illness that had cast a pall on the lives of every person in the United States."[3] *Big-C*: creativity that changes the world as we know it.

Lando taught at a high school where the culminating event and ultimate test of students' skills was the notorious senior thesis project, a scaled-down Master's thesis project that lasts an entire school year. One day, a student named Andy stayed after class to ask a question. He wanted to know if he could write a novella as his senior thesis. Lando felt terrible, knowing that the senior thesis couldn't possibly be a creative writing project. It was *inconceivable*. Andy began explaining his idea for the novella and his passion was palpable. In an effort to keep that fire lit, rather than dousing it with the rules and requirements of the thesis project, we began to ask *what if?* and started sketching on the whiteboard ways to shove a creative writing project into the traditional academic frame of the senior thesis. We asked ourselves, how can we achieve the aims of this daunting project and yet still pursue our passion for the novella? Andy helped his teacher see how something *could be* even though it didn't exist. In the end, Andy walked in to defend his thesis with a printed and bound copy of his novella, his signature work for his senior year. He broke the very game we designed for him to play. We had no idea that we had a signature thinker standing in front of us before we even had the term. The next year, because of his courage and risk-taking, other students traveled down the same creative path that Andy engineered, allowing others to ask *what if* and build prototypes of projects that have wowed us not by accident but by design. *little-c*: creativity that changes our daily, personal lives in meaningful ways.

Although the impact of the creative product is clearly different, these stories are quite similar. Both of the students actively took risks and asked *what if?* and were met by the status quo with either hostility or hesitation. Instead, we want to welcome our students' *what ifs?* and cultivate them through *Signature Thinking*. And our aim is not to create the next Salk. Rather, through constant exposure to *little-c* wins throughout their K12 experiences, students can store and stack these incremental victories and maybe—*just maybe*—one day experience a *Big-C* breakthrough.

So Who Can Be Creative?

Beghetto warns that "the way we and others talk about creativity can influence what our students believe about creativity."[4] Indeed, we must be mindful of the signals we are sending in our classroom about *what is* creative and *who can be* creative. David Burkus's book *The Myths of Creativity* systematically debunks the many longstanding misconceptions about creativity and creative people. One of the most pervasive and damaging myths is that there is a creative *breed* or *type*, usually associated with the tortured or eccentric artist. Too often, creativity is seen as frivolous play within the arts realm—whether it's a poem, an art piece, or a play. This is one of the reasons administrators, teachers, and parents shy away from creativity. The danger is twofold. First, we think, *creativity is an artist's game*, which isn't a worthy use of time. Second, we think, *I'm not an artist so I can't be creative*. Nothing could be farther from the truth.

Creativity rightfully includes poets, painters, and playwrights, but creativity is for *all*. During our creativity workshops, teachers are often shocked that they have believed in this myth for much of their lives—about themselves. A central office curriculum leader actually spoke to us after a workshop—through tears—that she has never considered herself creative because she never had an interest or aptitude in the arts. Once we shattered the *breed* myth, she began thinking of all the ways she is in fact creative, both in her personal life and how she coordinates curriculum at the district level. All humans have tremendous creative abilities, no matter the context or field of study. Thus, we need to take Hope and Wade King's advice from their book *The Wild Card*: widen our own view of *what is* creative and *who can be* creative in our classrooms. With enough practice and guidance, we can all—not just our students—unlock our latent creative capacities.

So Why Should You Be Creative?

Tony Wagner and Sir Ken Robinson have spent the past decade or more attempting to answer this question: What knowledge and skills will young people need in order to survive and thrive in the 21st-century global economy? A key result of their investigations was a set of non-negotiable skills, including critical thinking, entrepreneurialism, and agility and adaptability. Notice that they did not find compliance, obedience, and risk-aversion. Creativity, though, was the culminating skill on their lists.

Creativity is indeed the currency of the 21st century, and schools typically favor compliance and order over the risky results of creative thinking. Wagner rails against this antiquated mindset and warns in his books, documentaries, and keynotes that teaching creativity is an economic imperative. Dan Pink in his book *Drive* also warns that we are moving quickly toward an "economy that demands nonroutine, creative, conceptual abilities."[5] With the looming threat of automatization, young people need be able to not only do their jobs but also reinvent their jobs while they do them. Former presidential candidate Andrew Yang believes that a "tsunami of unemployment" is headed our way and that we must "expand what we think of as work."[6] Burkus notes that any company or organization wanting to stay "competitive in an innovation-driven economy needs creativity from every one of its people."[7] As teachers, we must take stock of these economic perils and ask: Are we helping students discover their innate gifts and helping hone them so that students can have a successful economic future?

Robinson, on the other hand, makes a different case for creativity: *joy*. The sheer joy one feels when creating or being creative is nonpareil to almost any other human endeavor. He laments that "many students think school is boring or distressing and as a result, an experience to be endured rather than enjoyed."[8] This is the opposite of what schools *could* and *should* be for students. Robinson's long crusade for joy in education is no frivolous act. Csikszentmihalyi's groundbreaking work revealed that when people are being creative they can often enter a state called *flow*, a heightened state of existence where time distorts itself and the ego fades as the joy of the task at hand completely arrests our energy and focus. We like to call it a *hot streak*. For us, we often experience hot streaks while writing (poetry for Lando; expository writing for Kevin). Others experience these sensations while gardening, exercising, or tinkering in the backyard shed. It is in these moments of *flow* that creative breakthroughs occur, and we want students to experience these joyous sensations within our classroom walls.

However, the *breed* myth that we mentioned earlier endures for many reasons and hinders our students' chances to enter *flow*. We must uproot the *breed* myth from our schools because it allows both adults and children to opt out of creative thinking. This not only lets them escape the discomfort of navigating uncertainty and risk-taking but also bars them from the richest, most complex thinking we can do as human beings. Fair warning: Students will need to do this type of thinking and imagining in order to meet the ever-changing demands of today's world. And to live *fully* is to live *creatively*, meaning that we must provide opportunities for students to experience the innate joy of creating. Opting out isn't an option.

So How Do We Do It?

We have so many reasons why we cannot afford to lose the creative capacity of any student. Students will undoubtedly need to find their own genius for both economic and personal well-being, and *Signature Thinking* demands it of them. We have built a framework that helps students uncover their latent creative talents, refine those talents, and experience the fruits of being creative. We help students develop those creative talents through iterative practice, collaboration, and reflection. Our framework tests those same talents through project-based learning. These real-world, urgency-laced projects force students to become action-oriented creators and innovators. The byproduct? *Signature Thinking*. The framework contains five interconnected elements that work together to cultivate creativity in the classroom (Figure 1.2). These elements are the collective key to unlocking productive creativity in your classroom and encouraging students to put their unique signatures on the work they do.

Signature Thinking
The Key to Classroom Creativity

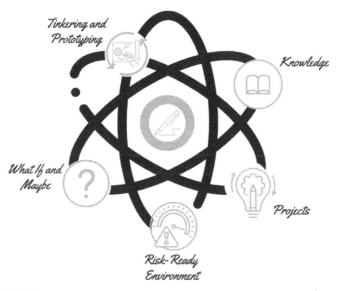

FIGURE 1.2

♦ *Signature Thinking Projects* (Chapter 2). Students deserve a curriculum that will help them uncover their *signatures* and share them with the world. This chapter helps teachers intentionally design a project-based curriculum that tips students toward creativity *by design*. We want to design real-world, action-oriented projects that first establish a *low floor*, meaning that all students can play our game. Next, we want projects with *wide-walls* that allow students to zig zag through our game by following both their passions and current skill levels. Finally, we want projects with *breakable ceilings*, meaning that we actively challenge students to break the very game we've designed for them to play in order for them to create striking, signature works.

♦ *Knowledge* (Chapter 3). We want students to *play*, but we also want them to *play well*. In order to think outside the box, they must first know the *depth* and *breadth* of the box so that they can press and sometimes even break the boundaries of the box. If we truly want to cultivate creativity in our classrooms, it begins with our commitment to equipping students with the knowledge needed for them to examine *what is* in order to dream of *what could be*.

♦ *Risk-Ready Environment* (Chapter 4). We set the conditions for creativity in the environments we engineer. The risk-ready environment welcomes risk-taking, failure, and trying again. Iteration and collaboration is the norm. We welcome students to challenge each other and us as well in order to learn, re-learn, and even un-learn.

♦ *The What if and Maybe Mindset* (Chapter 5). When students think and talk in what ifs and maybes they realize that they don't have to be *right, right now*. This mindset is a direct challenge to the culture of speed in K12 schools. Creative people know that the seeds of something special are born out of asking "what if" and embracing the uncomfortable uncertainty of maybes.

♦ *Tinkering and Prototyping* (Chapter 6). The most creative people in human history have several shared traits or behaviors. Some of them happen to be tinkering and building multiple models—both mental and physical—of their world-changing innovations. People who tinker understand that messiness, nonlinearity, and tons of tries are prerequisites to creative, signature breakthroughs.

♦ *Conclusion* (Chapter 7). *Signature Thinking* challenges all stakeholders—teachers, leaders, students, and parents—to think differently about what school could be. In this chapter, we address common concerns from the point of view of each stakeholder in order to make the case for creativity as a foundational piece of K12 schooling.

Conclusion

Although the *Signature Thinking* elements are presented sequentially, implementing *ST* happens much more messily. Sawyer would call it a *zig zag* path. The acquirement of knowledge, for example, is never limited to the beginning of the signature thinking process. Crucial knowledge must indeed be established first in order for students to play well. But knowledge will be built throughout the *ST* process as students learn to talk in *what ifs* and *maybes*. The what if and maybe mindset, likewise, is a crucial precursor to successful tinkering and prototyping. These what ifs are often tested within the wide walls of projects through tinkering and building prototypes, but these elements occur throughout the entire signature thinking process in cyclical, non-linear ways. Even the designing of creative curriculum happens in unexpected ways. Teachers, as the architects of creative learning experiences, often ask during the project planning phase: What if we learned to tell time this way? What if we studied *Macbeth* that way? Or, the creative architect might ask in the midst of the project: What if we added this to the project? What if we stopped the project in order to play in another domain that is surprisingly needed now in order for students to enhance their creativity? Thus, we caution our readers about the linear presentation of the *ST* elements. Students' signatures are born in the *fusion* of these elements, and implementation is messy, nonlinear, and takes time. So we must ask ourselves: How willing are *we* to *zig zag* alongside students through the twists and turns of signature thinking? Because it starts with us.

Notes

1   Beghetto, *Beautiful Risks*, p. 95
2   Amabile, *Big C, Little C, Howard, and Me: Approaches to Understanding Creativity.*
3   Csikszentmihalyi, *Creativity*, p. 282
4   Beghetto, *Beautiful Risks*, p. 17
5   Pink, *Drive*, p. 95
6   Yang, *Realtime*, 2019
7   Burkus, *Myths of Creativity*, p. 48
8   Robinson, *Creative Schools*, p. 134

2

Signature Thinking Projects

Wiggins and McTighe changed the way countless teachers viewed themselves with their seminal work *Understanding by Design*. Teachers, after reading their work, often come to see themselves as designers and architects of learning experiences. Essentially, they see that learning by luck is too big a chance to take. For creativity in the classroom, we take that same approach in that we design—purposefully and intentionally—learning experiences for students to not only discover their latent creative talents but also cultivate those talents for a lifelong pursuit of both skill and joy. It is not by chance that students are creative; the *Signature Thinking* framework demands it of them.

So how do we design *for* creativity in the classroom? Our lesson plans can either fuel or drain creativity. It's a design choice that starts with us. We want our students to fall into creativity. And to avoid the overwhelming anxiety of needing to start from scratch, Ronald Beghetto says to start looking for small openings for creativity in our current curriculum. This chapter will help us find those openings and take small steps toward designing signature thinking projects.

DOI: 10.4324/9781003201380-2

So Why Projects?

When we work with teachers to design curricular experiences for students, we always ask an uncomfortable question: are you *designing* and *assigning* work worth doing? Work worthy of students' signatures? The crowd often bristles because it forces them to reflect upon their curricular designs as well as what George Couros asks in *The Innovator's Mindset*: Would we want to be students in our own classes? Students not only *deserve* but also *need* a creative curriculum—for their livelihood and their quality of life:

> Creative thinking has always been, and will always be, a central part of what makes life worth living. Life as a creative thinker can bring not only economic rewards, but also joy, fulfillment, purpose, and meaning. Children deserve nothing less.
>
> Mitchel Resnick[1]

Remember, humans are designed for creative thinking and creative output, but the monotony of school often deadens students' craving to create and works against our natural wiring to challenge, to subvert, and to take risks. Ken Robinson and Mitchel Resnick both warn that we may have even destroyed the innate joy and passion of kindergarten! Tony Wagner, likewise, rails against the drudgery and school and lack of student autonomy and motivation, especially at the high school level. However, these problems—even if they are sometimes overstated—are real and solvable. We are not too far gone to reclaim passion and engagement in schools. Therefore, we must have a curriculum that aligns with students' passions and encourages their natural promethean inclinations. We want to create an army of fire starters.

We meet this challenge head-on through designing and assigning real-world projects that help students to develop their signatures. We want to capture the urgency of real-world work through the most common type of work that occurs in the real world: projects! Almost every field operates in a project-based system, and these projects include multiple, non-linear paths toward multiple ways of being *right*.

Wagner's work reveals that young people will need a number of *survival skills* in order to be successful in the fast-paced, unpredictable world of tomorrow. Among those necessary skills are *agility and adaptability*, meaning that students will need to consistently and actively navigate ambiguities, disruptions, and multiple ways to solve problems. James Stronge, author of *Qualities of Effective Teachers*, notes that "Twenty-first century students need to be able to confront complex ethical questions, engage in productive dialogues across ideological divides, and decide among imperfect options."[2] In other words, compliance won't cut it anymore. So, how agile and adaptable are we—as the designers—in our own classrooms? How willing are we to toss a lesson plan and build projects out of headlines? Project-based learning is messy, but it is a *necessity*.

So What Is a Signature Thinking Project?

Our passion for projects was inspired by many, but Resnick's blueprint for projects from *Lifelong Kindergarten* was particularly impactful. He asks teachers to consider designing projects first with *low floors*, meaning that any student can play the game we've created irrespective of background knowledge or socioeconomic challenges or any other barrier in front of students. With the *low floor* concept for projects, students can enter at their own speed—much like a gamer can select a difficulty level on the start-up screen. Similar to a Role Playing Game (RPG), students with more prior knowledge or experience or equipment can enter our game a bit faster, but all students can still explore the world we've created at their own pace, pursuing what intrigues them and challenges them on a personal level.

While they are exploring, students will then encounter—by design—the *wide walls* of the game we've created for them. Resnick wants students to luxuriate inside the content, problems, tasks, and challenges of a project. All students will enter the *low floor* but then will be encouraged to explore on a solo mission or perhaps they organically find a team to join on a crusade to complete the project. Teachers will *willingly* encourage students to *zig zag* throughout the project space as they discover, play, and encounter roadblocks. The notion of projects with *wide walls* also means that teachers are willing to accept products, outputs, and creations that could be different for each student or team while at the same time offering guarantees that certain standards and skills are met by design. This symbiotic loose and tight project design ensures both student engagement and student mastery of non-negotiable skills. For instance, in a project focused on mastering speaking and listening skills for an ELA class, some students may show their mastery of skills through a live presentation with visual aids while another set of students create a video or hold a town hall debate in class. We, as the designers of learning experiences, have *planned for* such customization and in fact welcome it in the culmination of student products and creations.

This brings us to the final design element of our project framework: *breakable ceilings*. This is the area where we pivot from Resnick's blueprint. Instead of designing projects with *high ceilings*, we challenge teachers to design projects with *breakable ceilings*. Projects with high ceilings help students soar, and adding the notion of a *breakable ceiling* encourages students to shatter the game we've built for them to play. In fact, we are *asking* for them to break our game to allow them to experience *signature thinking*, where students create products that are not only innovative and creative but also so customized that they can put their signature on them. Think about students who have completely shocked us when they submit their work. We often wonder *how did they do this*? But we will be surprised at what students will do *if we let them*. However, there are also times when students break ceilings and get punished for innovation and creativity. Think about students who beat our rubrics and checklists by creating something *better* than what we'd planned for, something that gave us everything we asked for and *more*. Often, we aren't sure how to assess such innovations and creations, but with a design mindset of projects with breakable ceilings (Figure 2.1),

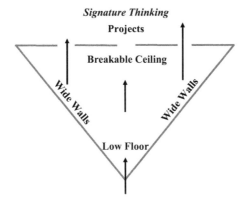

FIGURE 2.1

we are apt and ready to embrace students who take risks and break our games not by *chance* but by *design* and thereby experience the transformative power of signature thinking.

Projects that Foster Collaboration

Students will also need help beyond us in order to become *signature thinkers*. They will need their peers. Just like Wagner and Stronge warn, exploring non-linear pathways and the nuances of real-world problems can be overwhelming. That's why we need projects that utilize effective collaborative teaming. Wagner, Robinson, and Resnick all agree that students will need to leverage each other's skills in order to have innovative breakthroughs. In fact, the world's greatest and most enduring breakthroughs have come from teams working on projects while under intense constraints.

Burkus expertly dispels "Lone Creator Myth" his book *The Myths of Creativity*. It turns out Edison did indeed test countless filaments before landing on the right one for the lightbulb, but it also turns out that he didn't do it alone; he had a team. Likewise, Prince will always be known as a lone virtuoso, but he collaborated with *The Revolution* and several brilliant sound engineers to craft his instantly recognizable, signature sound.

The story, however, is more compelling if a sole genius worked tirelessly alone to change the world. But nothing could be farther from the truth. We want to honor the longstanding tradition of creative collaboration within our curricular designs.

Think about bands, athletic teams, military units, think tanks, and even comedy duos. All of these teams work together to creatively find and solve problems within the source code of their domains. And guess what? The best teams are diverse in thought, background, and talent. Remember Edison? He had a team of interdisciplinary tinkerers who helped him change the world. Keith Sawyer in his book *Zig Zag* recounts that the double helix team shared expertise in biology, x-ray crystallography, and physics. And these expert teams don't always agree, and that's a good thing for creativity. Burkus debunks the "Cohesion Myth" in his book as well, noting that the best teams, whether its Pixar or IDEO, are incredibly diverse and leverage that diversity to create productive conflict. So we want to engineer experiences where students can dive into complex projects and generate novel solutions with intentional friction. This means students don't always get to work with their friends or people with like minds. As designers, we want to stack our teams with opposites in order to inculcate a sense of divergent thinking in our classrooms. John and Paul of *The Beatles*. Paul and Gene of *KISS*.

Start small. Show students a way to solve a math problem and then have them work in teams to create two or more novel ways to solve it, ways only their team could come up with. Design an engineering lesson that demands students sketch multiple prototypes in order to dream up different solutions. In an ELA class, analyze a chapter from a book or a play and then ask groups to analyze that same chapter from a minor character's perspective. According to Csikszentmihalyi, being able to see and then un-see from different vantage points is a signature of creative thinkers.[3] A sixth grader once told me during a small group discussion on heroes and villains that the Joker was his favorite bad guy. I asked him, *"what if* he's not a villain?" Their brains almost melted when they discovered the notion of the *anti-hero*. So to help students make this type of contrarian thinking the new normal, have them team up to explore the ambiguities of the content. Once both we and our students are ready, we can challenge them with the signature thinking projects embedded throughout this book.

Projects that Promote Fusion

Collaboration on projects is also a way for students to experience another creativity touchstone: *fusion*. Almost all innovative, breakthrough ideas come from fusing genres or domains together in new and useful ways. We mentioned *KISS* earlier. They set out to create the band they never saw by improvising on *The Beatles'* use of four individual identities, fused with the theatrics of an Alice Cooper show. The result? Something we'd never seen or heard before. In 1988, when Motley Crue and Poison were at the peak of their musical impact, Nirvana was already creating the underground sound that would only a few years later destroy a decade of music. Nirvana's signature sound was more than just different from the hair kings of L.A.; it also captured an inconceivable mixture of audiences. This collaborative team asked: *What if* we could create a sound that unites our underground audience with mainstream rockers? Record companies took the risk and Nirvana knocked the world on its heels. The arts are ripe for these types of creative fusion, but remember that fusion can happen in *all* areas.

At High Tech High, for example, the innovative school at the center of the documentary *Most Likely to Succeed*, teachers actively merge physics with the humanities to help students collaboratively blend domains and make novel connections. At the Stanford d.school, Tina Seelig has her students practicing the very same multidisciplinary fusion because Silicon Valley companies are hungry for the next innovative idea:

> Very innovative companies, such as Twitter, know how important this type of cross-pollination is to creativity in

their businesses, and they make an effort to hire people with unusual skills, knowing that diversity of thinking will certainly influence the development of their products.[4]

And this hunger isn't limited to STEM fields. The Duffner brothers, the duo behind the hit Netflix series *Stranger Things*, fused elements of *ET*, *IT*, *The Goonies*, *The Monster Squad*, and *Stand by Me* in order to produce something simultaneously nostalgic *and* novel; in essence: something truly creative.

Thus, it is crucial to intentionally design curricular experiences that leverage *crosstalk* and *cross-pollination* to allow for fusion to occur. We want students to have ready access to materials and ideas from different domains so that they can be constantly on the lookout for inconceivable connections and combinations.[5] And thankfully we don't need to be at the d.school or Apple to practice fusion. We can practice at our own schools with the existing materials we have. It could be as simple as designing an interdisciplinary project where classes search for meaningful connections in the textbooks. For example, a fusion of English and Psychology. A colleague from the psychology department came by Lando's English class one day and asked if he knew of any short stories about psychopaths. Lando knew just the story they needed. They joined classes and collaboratively read and studied "A Good Man is Hard to Find" by Flannery O'Conner. The depth of conversation, the connections made, and the engagement from this week-long project were incredible. Or, an example from Kevin's History class and a fusion of history and science. A colleague teaching physics one year lined up his instruction of nuclear fission to parallel the United States' history courses' exploration of the Cold War. This deep dive into the awesome and frightening power of nuclear energy was richer and deeper than it had been in the past. In both history and physics, students explored the incredible benefits of nuclear power to mankind but also the risks associated with this *Big-C* breakthrough. The project culminated in a series of debates over nuclear power considering its benefits and drawbacks, leaving students with a unique contribution to the understanding of how science and history are interwoven to varied audiences. Both of these became perennial projects and student favorites.

Burkus reminds us that *creativity is a team sport*,[6] and that includes students collaborating, asking *what if*, and cross-pollinating ideas with their teachers. Beghetto asks us all to team up so that everyone can get acclimated to the new normal of creative thinking in our classrooms.

> As you become more confident with making openings in your assignments and activities, you and your students can push out the walls of possibility and raise the ceiling on what students are asked to do.[7]

In many ways, we are asking students and teachers to *unlearn* what they know about school and learning itself. So we must be patient and pace ourselves. Then, with more practice and creative confidence of our own, we can take larger curricular leaps toward signature thinking projects that promote collaboration and fusion.

Projects that Help Us Slow Down and Get Farther

All of the ideas we've presented thus far to design *for* creativity will fail if we don't *slow down*. We must challenge the culture of speed in our school system. From Salk to Springsteen, we know that creative breakthroughs happen when you try and try again. Salk didn't create the polio vaccine overnight, and Springsteen didn't record *Born to Run* in a day either. We must let students *zig zag* through their learning experiences and build multiple prototypes through the tinkering process. Most important, we must align both our mindsets and grade books to these creative conditions. When students don't have to be *right, right now* and are invited—and, at times, required—to try and try again without penalty, they will build the creative confidence and endurance needed to have signature breakthroughs.

Let's explore real-world examples of innovators and creators taking their time and experiencing *flow*. Think about one of Michelangelo's signature works: David. He likely didn't create David in 50-minute bursts, once a day, five days a week. Instead, it took countless hours, and he was a master of his craft. Think about Prince, who was known for marathon recording sessions that lasted days. Sound engineers would work with him in revolving shifts because they couldn't run the booth for days at a time without sleep. Prince, on the other hand, was unstoppable once in flow. Think about Key and Peele, who produced some of the most iconic and provocative comedy sketches of today and how it took writing five times the sketches needed and eight months of tinkering and prototyping to get those signature sketches to the screen. Robinson puts it plainly in his book *Creative Schools*: "If every forty or so minutes, the whole workforce had to stop what it was doing, move to different rooms, do something else entirely, and rinse and repeat six times a day, the business would rapidly grind to a halt."[8]

We want to design projects that mirror the conditions in which real-world creators and innovators operate and experience flow; we want to design projects that allow students to explore and luxuriate inside the content, problems, and tasks within our game. Csikszentmihalyi spent years studying the behaviors of creative individuals, and they do not rush to find their signature; it often takes decades of exploration and dabbling.[9] School, if we let it, could become the kick-starter for students' long and winding quest to discovering their passions and talents. Thus, we must slow down and let students feed their passions by carving out time to get lost in learning.

However, we only have so much time with students each day, and this time is often not as protected as we'd prefer. The roadblocks to slowing down to allow for flow include our bell schedules, lack of autonomy, or the pressures of standardized tests. These are real barriers, but we also can't make excuses. Hope and Wade King say that we are the *wildcards* for students; students are counting on us to be *a little bit different*; to fight through the structural challenges and make creativity a part of students' daily lives. In a world where we have little time to contemplate, meditate, reflect, and create, our classrooms will stand as the last bastions of hope to help students find their signatures.

Conclusion

From Wagner's *Creating Innovators* to Csikszentmihalyi's *Creativity*, the impact of the teacher on student creativity is clear. Renowned creators and innovators repeatedly report that individual teachers—not school in itself—were the ones who often *noticed* and then *cultivated* their passion and thinking. Those teachers then *mentored* them to a level where they could successfully exhibit their work—whether it was at a poetry night or a science expo. The role of the teacher, one who can see students' latent, unrefined signatures, is a recurring take-away from the research on how the world's most creative people got creative. Thus, we must remember that creating signature thinkers in the classroom undoubtedly starts with us. Here is a list of design tips that to help us become catalysts for creativity:

- ◆ Design and assign work worth doing.
- ◆ Create urgency through real-world projects.
- ◆ Provide opportunities for coaching and feedback on creative ideas and approaches.
- ◆ Simultaneously coach and critique students as they create and innovate.
- ◆ Align students with like and unlike teammates and mentors to foster contrarian thinking.
- ◆ Help students *fuse* ideas by facilitating links between and across disciplines.
- ◆ Walk alongside students as they ask *what if?* and tinker.
- ◆ Create alongside students and seek their input, feedback, and coaching.

The last two tips, which we will dig deeper into in the next chapters, are especially crucial to cultivating classroom creativity.

Even with all of these design components and mindsets in place, it won't amount to much if students don't see us as active creators as well. Leveraging these traits sends signals that creativity is something that we all do—even the teacher. And the creative teacher also loves to ask *what if?* and tinker too. Mo Willems, author of the Elephant and Piggie book series, says that children "will create if they see the adults around them creating."[10] We must model creative thinking and creative actions on a daily basis. Ask, during the next team or faculty meeting, how often do our students see us being creative? And discuss ways to take risks, tinker, build prototypes, share unfinished work, and seek feedback from students on how we can amplify our own creativity. If they have to write an essay, write one with them. If they have to build a diorama, build one too. The myth is that we either need to get in or out of students' way, whether it's to deposit knowledge or encourage freethinking. In truth, we must walk alongside students.

Signature Thinking Project Checklist

Does your project have a *low floor*? meaning that *all* students have the necessary knowledge/skills to play the game and *play well*.	Notes:
☐	
Does your project have *wide walls*? meaning that the products/outputs/results could look different in the end.	Notes:
☐	

Signature Thinking **Project Checklist (cont.)**

Does your project have a breakable
ceiling?
meaning that you have prepared for
and designed for students to break the
game.

Notes:

☐

Are students collaborating with
each other and with teachers to gain
knowledge, receive feedback, and
practice contrarian thinking?

Notes:

☐

Does your project promote fusion so
that students can make links between
and across disciplines?

Notes:

☐

Are your students being given enough
time to *tinker* and *prototype* in order to
create multiple models?

Notes:

☐

Are you walking alongside students
as they ask *what if?* and tinker? Are
you creating alongside students and
seeking their input, feedback, and
coaching on your own creative works?

Notes:

☐

Notes

1   Resnick, *Lifelong Kindergarten*, p. 6
2   Stronge, *Qualities of Effective Teachers*, p. 119
3   Csikszentmihalyi, *Creativity*, p. 365
4   Seelig, *Ingenius*, pp. 42–43
5   Sawyer, *Zig Zag*, p. 7
6   Burkus, *Myths of Creativity*, p. 117
7   Beghetto, *Beautiful Risks*, p. 58
8   Robinson, *Creative Schools*, p. 91
9   Csikszentmihalyi, *Creativity*, p. 370
10 Martin, "Kids' Author Mo Willems Has a New Creative Challenge"

3

Knowledge—The Key to Playing Well

Now that we've got you excited about a creative curriculum, we must provide this warning: students must *know* before they can challenge the status quo. It is not uncommon for people to say that building knowledge and memorizing key facts is detrimental to creativity. It is true that overemphasis on holding knowledge as the sole aim can stifle creativity. However, the research is clear. Creative thinking and all forms of productive creativity rest upon a rich knowledge base. Furthermore, a broad base of knowledge—that is, information memorized that can be harnessed from and applied to a wide spectrum of domains is also crucial. Cultivating creativity in our classrooms begins with a commitment to equipping students with essential knowledge that bears on the topic being examined as well as a broader knowledge base from which they can reexamine and reimagine the topic under study through new and varied lenses. If we want to leverage creativity to make learning more meaningful, more engaging, and more enduring, we cannot begin without explicit attention being paid to knowledge. We want to equip our students not to merely *play* but to *play well*.

DOI: 10.4324/9781003201380-3

Advocates for creativity who champion *play* as the primary vehicle for creativity too often sidestep the role knowledge plays in *playing well*. In his book *Lifelong Kindergarten*, Mitchel Resnick details his long tenure as both an MIT professor and collaborator with the LEGO company. He notes that the word *lego* literally means to *play well*, and that's always been the company's mission. To live this mission in the classroom, a deep knowledge base must be established before students can think critically in an effective manner and then successfully produce novel and useful ideas and innovations. The best comedians, for example, know not only what came *before* them but also *how* and *why* it happened that way. The stand-up comedy special wasn't always a hallmark format for comedians. It was born out of the comedy club scene and codified as the apex of a performer's career when Richard Pryor sold out Madison Square Garden. Pryor set the standard for the format, then Murphy played jazz with it, then Kinison yelled at the audience, and then Seinfeld wondered *what the deal was*. Each were able to both fit in *and* stick out, bending and stretching the very format of the stand-up special. Expert comedians know the tangled and non-linear history of their field, and they also know that the stand-up special was just one of many movements in their diverse domain. This simultaneous depth and breadth of comedy knowledge—from stand-ups to sit-coms—allows them to synthesize what's been done and purposefully pivot from it to create their own *signature*. Likewise, this undergirding of diverse knowledge in a domain is crucial to students' success in becoming creative thinkers who bend the boundaries of that same domain—and sometimes even break it.

How Can Knowledge Be Harnessed to Promote Creativity?

As we discussed in the introduction chapter, truly creative works are not just novel or original; they also *work* and do so in a particular context. So before students engage with the elements of signature thinking, we must ensure that they have the knowledge they need to succeed. Being creative is hard work, and it takes a lot of knowledge to be truly creative. One of the most pervasive misconceptions surrounding creativity, as Burkus explains in *The Myths of Creativity*, is that innovative ideas arrive out of nowhere or in *eureka* moments. This myth undercuts the tremendous knowledge-base and expertise needed to be successfully creative and often feeds a false sense of creativity capacity among novices.

When we begin to harness the power of knowledge in cultivating creativity, we must first clearly identify the essential knowledge students must have before playing our game. Two questions can guide us to clarify essential knowledge: (1) What is necessary to know to succeed during this learning experience? (2) What knowledge is so important for later learning that its mastery makes it essential? Wiggins and McTighe in their book *Understanding by Design* use the following process to help determine what students must know now and what can be known along the way through play (Figure 3.1).

Similarly, we use a card sorting strategy that helps us determine far in advance what students must know in order to play well (Figure 3.2). With your collaborative team or teaching partner, write down on the cards all of the key knowledge and standards students must know before starting the unit or project. Then, sort the cards into hierarchies of *must know now* and *can know as they go*.

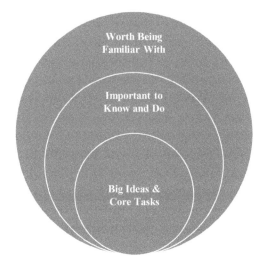

FIGURE 3.1

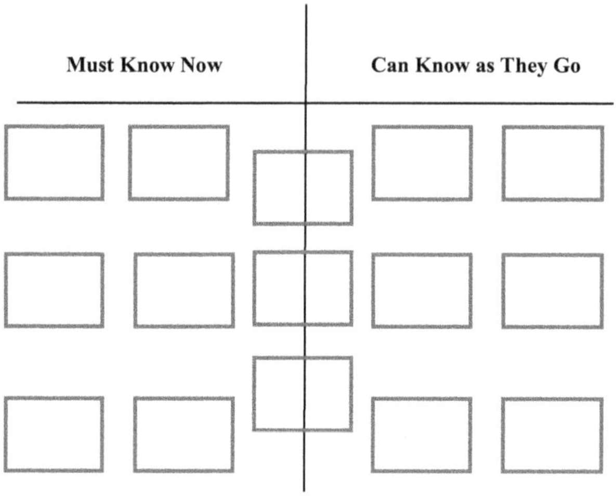

Must Know Now			Can Know as They Go	
☐	☐	☐	☐	☐
☐	☐	☐	☐	☐
☐	☐	☐	☐	☐

FIGURE 3.2

Ensuring that the teacher is clear on these non-negotiable learnings helps maximize creative potential because we can then commit to guaranteeing that every single student will know the essential material needed to start the unit or project and that he or she will have—by design—stored it in their long-term memory by the end.

Once we have clarified exactly what is *essential*, we must reflect upon this question: Is this knowledge or skill essential in order to play the game or is it essential to get somewhere along the way? For all those things that simply must be in place before diving in, it becomes a stop sign for us, as the architects of learning experiences. We must guarantee that every single student in our class has this essential knowledge in place *before* we launch. For all those things that are necessary but not essential in order to get started, we need a series of pause points throughout our learning experiences that allow students to navigate through a path of their own choosing but with carefully placed check-ins that ensure this auxiliary knowledge is in place. In doing this we guarantee that every learner not only plays our game (learning experience, activity, project, etc.) but that they can play well. If we want them to experience creative breakthroughs, it is playing well that matters; not merely playing.

Should We Focus on Breadth or Depth?

Next, we must help our students develop a reservoir of diverse knowledge from which they can draw, providing them with both *breadth* across disciplines, perspectives, and eras and *depth* within the core area under study. Poet Marcus Jackson teaches his apprentices to read *across eras* in order to see the signatures of poets from a macro lens so that they can one day *fuse* techniques, styles, and structures across eras while also adding their own poetic signatures. Echoing this sort of sentiment, another famous poet, T.S. Eliot, argued for the importance of having knowledge of our collective past. It is this way with all domains; if we only know what is typical today we will remain myopic. We want our students to look beyond a fixation on the present, and building a broad knowledge base is one of the best ways to do this. Doing so enables students to see connections that others would miss; to examine issues beyond a silo; and to imagine the possibilities and ask *what if?* To a large extent creativity is about discovering the elegant patterns of meaning across diverse, seemingly unrelated ideas and domains. Without a broad knowledge base from which those patterns can be recognized, students will struggle to discover these patterns and make novel connections. David Epstein, in his book *Range*, found something similar in studying the world's most successful leaders in various fields: in particular, he found that generalists excel, especially when the field is complex and unpredictable.[1] Encouraging students to reexamine topics through deliberate interaction with areas beyond the one at hand helps them to imagine what is possible and what *could be*. Additionally, creativity is incremental—that is our capacity to express creative thoughts builds over time while working in a domain. Classrooms framed around an unending battle between knowledge and imagination challenge students to talk in *what ifs* and *maybes*, tipping them toward *signature thinking*.

Broad knowledge alone is, however, insufficient to truly prepare students for creative thinking and learning. Students also must be challenged to dive *deeply* into specific ideas, genres, and topics and examine these areas in richer complexity; meanwhile, through this development of deeper understanding, students also develop an awareness of the vast knowledge at play in a particular domain. These deep dives will cultivate a desire for students to know more, driving their curiosity as they examine topics that they once had a basic understanding of and, upon the deep dive, leave with new eyes open to the vastness of those topics. This cultivation of deep knowledge is a necessary counterpart to the broad knowledge building. When combined, students imagine possibilities that are not just novel but that are intriguing and worthy of further exploration.

As teachers, we ensure that students are equipped with sufficient knowledge across a broad range of domains so they can successfully and innovatively *fuse* domains together. Breadth, not depth, is the key to *seeing* inconceivable[2] connections and thereby making novel linkages that are truly creative. We also want our students to develop an appreciation for the grit and determination it takes to develop a deep understanding within a domain by providing opportunities for targeted, iterative examinations of topics. Knowledge building, whether breadth or depth, is not a one and done endeavor; it takes *time*. However, in our culture of speed we cannot feasibly read and study everything from all domains. So, we strive for a breadth-depth balance, one that simultaneously offers broad exposure and deliberate deep dives into significant topics, one that allows students to imagine possibilities beyond *what is* and the competence to pursue *what could be*—the fulcrum of signature thinking.

How Do We Fuse Knowledge-Building and Creativity?

A powerful false dichotomy exists among teachers and how they should deliver knowledge to students. On one hand, we are tempted to stand in front of students and deposit knowledge into their heads—what Freire mockingly called the *banking method*. On the other, we are tempted to walk away and let students play and explore freely without bounds. The truth is that we need to strike a balance between getting *in* or *out* of students' way. We need to, consequently, walk *alongside* students through their thinking, learning, and creating. This blend of teaching, coaching, and mentoring allows students to receive the benefits of all these approaches: directed modeling, guided practicing, and reciprocated learning.

For many teachers, shifting from a knowledge deliverer to a knowledge facilitator is a challenge. Once teachers determine first what students must know in order to be successful in the upcoming project, they can then determine what knowledge can be learned along the way, along the learning journey, which forces the teacher to walk alongside students through apprenticeship opportunities. We should engage in creative expression *together* so that students receive the proper modeling and guided practice they need to thrive on their own. We should encourage students to mirror the master teacher, as Barton Kunstler notes, because "creativity has everything to do with copying and repetition. Absorbing lessons from the masters is an incredibly efficient way to learn the most powerful techniques."[3] However, Kunstler says we shouldn't stop there; students must go beyond copying. Resnick also warns us about the pitfalls of mimicry in *Lifelong Kindergarten*:

> As students go through school, they often experience teaching as the delivery of instruction ("Do this, do that") and the delivery of information ("Here's what you need to know")...this approach to teaching can be de-motivating for many learners. What's more, this approach steers learners away from the types of creative experimentation that is so important in today's world, leading them to imitate rather than innovate.[4]

Indeed, as students' depth and breadth of knowledge expands and sharpens as they play, we then press them to openly and frequently challenge the master and the very game we've built for them. This is how we help students leverage knowledge *and* play to become signature thinkers. We honor the time it takes to build that knowledge and lean into knowledge-building so that we can challenge conventional wisdom *when the time is right*.

The Ballpark

Suzie Boss offers great advice in getting a project started and how to uncover what knowledge students currently have as well as the knowledge they need: "Early in the project, a variety of strategies—including concept maps, know-wonder-learn charts, online surveys, and whole-class discussion—will help you discover what prior knowledge students bring to the topic."[5] *The Ballpark* exercise is one of our signature brainstorming exercises that helps students see how much they need to know before attempting creative thinking. As we've mentioned, we want our students to not only play but to play well, and you can't play well without knowing *how* to play in a particular context or domain. However, there are caveats to brainstorming activities, one being that simply gathering people to a white board to unload a host of ideas will not, by itself, yield creative breakthroughs. Indeed, brainstorming alone won't help us break ceilings, but the process done in an iterative and layered fashion with proper coaching will.

The Ballpark process begins with framing the context and problem at hand. This process works for any discipline or age group and helps establish the essential knowledge and *low floor*, allowing all students to participate regardless of varied levels of background knowledge or skills. Whether we're discussing the scientific method with elementary school students or the generational differences with high school seniors, it works.

Once we frame the context and problem, we place a keyword or phrase in the center of a whiteboard or a large piece of butcher paper (Figure 3.3). Then, we ask students to mark up the board or paper with everything they think goes inside the ballpark or conversation about the scientific method (testing, hypothesis, beakers) or the generations (history, hobbies, politics, biases).

FIGURE 3.3

We want anything and everything put on the white board that is potentially relevant. We think of this as starting by casting the widest net possible because very often, our first idea is not our best idea. But all too often we stop at our first idea. The ballpark exercise simultaneously shows students the vastness of the conversation and problem under study and the need to be knowledgeable before attempting to innovate. It also provides students—and the teacher—with a record of their thinking as a group and as individuals while they cycle through the Ballpark maps together and while they make their own. This physical record of their thinking lays the groundwork of a rich and broad knowledge base. This established groundwork can then help free up students' working memory within the actual project so that they can truly exercise the higher order demands of creative thinking. Subsequently, we could have students categorize everything the ballpark to start to "see" patterns within the central topic and our collective thinking. This can be used to help zero in on areas to focus on for a project or areas to build knowledge because we can see the vastness of what we need to know.

The Ballpark allows students to store their new knowledge from this exercise through revisiting ideas again and again to get something novel. This takes time as student learn, unlearn, and relearn within our wide walled projects that could take two weeks or two months to complete. This process also allows teachers to see students' prior knowledge on a topic or area as well as gaps in thinking or misconceptions early in the project. The Ballpark serves as a versatile formative check, allowing the architects to make in the moment adjustments to the learning and project plans to come. This allows teachers to intervene and correct course immediately and direct the class toward learning aims that are more advanced or recognize that more time may be needed to build essential background knowledge before marching ahead. With this rich data, we can also help students successfully navigate the intentional ambiguities embedded into the unit or project by drawing upon the classifications uncovered and pointing out connections among them.

Having completed the foundational goals of the ballpark activity, our class is now primed for debate, discussion, and sparring over ideas. Together, we cycle through problems and solutions as we constantly revisit throughout learning to promote renegotiation of ideas, reclassification of ideas, and reconsideration of items seen *and* unseen, recognition of caricatures or limited understandings earlier. All this helps facilitate an environment in which connections are built and strengthened. It is widely acknowledged that getting it right the first time is not the most important thing. And since developing a more accurate understanding takes time and reflection, this process facilitates both creative capacity and learning that endures for the long term.

The Ballpark strategy provides a non-linear pathway for students to develop novel ideas that not only work but also work in a specific context. Adding on something or extending an idea in a way that does not have practical or theoretical relevance is not something we are seeking to cultivate. It has to be novel, but it also has to work. Productive creativity is exemplified by flexibility, originality, and elaboration. In terms of each, their creative expression rests upon context and then the imagining of novel and achievable possibilities. Flexible thinking is illustrated by working with change. Being able to recognize change requires knowledge of what was *before* so as to dream of what *could be* instead in the future. Working alongside their peers and the master teacher through the Ballpark, students can traverse these challenges in a safe and supportive environment.

Conclusion

Here's the big idea: students must *know* before they can challenge the status quo. Knowledge is not at odds with creativity; rather, it is the essential foundation from which productive creativity emerges and flourishes. For another example, Tim Burton loved bad movies as a kid; he studied them, realizing that he could see the signature hidden within, but the movies didn't quite work.

Yet the Hollywood formula was also so unfulfilling—creatively—to Burton. And through years of studying the craft and tinkering, Burton was able to strike a balance between weird *and* Warner Brothers, hence aligning with the research definition of creativity: it's novel, and it works. After 30 years of subverting what movies and stories can and could be, Tim Burton's signature is now unmistakable.

Educators must cultivate creativity that is useful and productive, and we do this by first ensuring that a foundational knowledge-base is in place. Then we provide meaningful opportunities for our students to talk in *what ifs* and *maybes*, allowing students to imagine the possibilities through iterative exploration of topics at increasing depths and from different lenses. The core processes for creative expression are reimagining, renegotiating, revisiting, revising, and building from information we have. Indeed, creativity includes both *fitting in* and *sticking out*. Such ability to both recognize the limits of what is possible and to identify meaningful opportunities to stretch or break those boundaries are predicated on one's knowledge-base. Within the classroom then, we must reflect on how knowledge in our domain can be leveraged to cultivate rather than to crush creativity. Reflect upon the following questions as the architects of learning. First, do our students know enough to *play* and *play well*? Second, how often are students encouraged to demonstrate knowledge and then challenge that very knowledge in order to become *signature thinkers*?

Notes

1 Epstein, *Range*.
2 Cronin and Loewenstein, in their book *The Craft of Creativity*, note that the ability to move from what is inconceivable to conceivable is a requisite skill in making creative breakthroughs.
3 Kunstler, *The Hothouse Effect*, p. 74.
4 Resnick, *Lifelong Kindergarten*, p. 111.
5 Boss, *Implementing PBL*, p. 58.

4

Risk-Ready Environment

Remember, classroom creativity can happen *by* design if we explicitly search for those creative openings in our curriculum. This same mindset also extends beyond curriculum to the learning environment itself. In fact, we set the conditions for creativity in the environments we engineer. We challenge teachers and students to celebrate the near-miss and the second and third attempt. We welcome errors, and as Hattie[1] notes, view them as powerful opportunities to learn. Innovative and creative thinking is messy, non-linear, and time intensive; iteration and collaboration is a must. The world is *wicked*, as David Epstein outlines in his book *Range*, and full of *wicked* problems. This means that the real world is flooded with problems that are ill-defined, unlike a chess game with *kind* rules. And each problem is different, laced with contextual and environmental nuances that weren't present on the previous project. This time there's a new team, a new scenario, a new budget—all new *constraints*. Thus, we want to prepare our students for this wicked world where they can practice navigating ambiguity, analyzing conflicting data, and persisting through complex challenges. We embrace this

DOI: 10.4324/9781003201380-4

wickedness and uncertainty and leverage creative thinking as the antidote. We also actively push back against the culture of speed in K12 schools. We welcome students to challenge each other and us in order to learn, re-learn, and even un-learn. These are the signatures of a *Risk-Ready Environment*.

Step 1—Slow Down

The incubation period, where the mind is actively not thinking about the problem or project under study, is imperative to creative breakthroughs. According to Sawyer, there's no "creativity without some slack time. This is one of the most solid findings of creativity research."[2] In a world with little time to contemplate, meditate, debrief or reflect, how can we provide the crucial incubation period students need to process ideas and make novel connections? Students deserve the chance to savor the content and think of unique ways to add their signatures to the projects and problems we present them. Challenging the culture of speed and linear learning in K12 schools was one of Sir Ken Robinson's lifelong pursuits, and the risk-ready environment achieves these goals with both mindset and strategy shifts that work. The first step in building such an environment is to *slow down*. However, a willful acknowledgment that this is no overnight endeavor is crucial to our success. It takes sustained commitment to the antithesis of many traditional ways K12 schools operate. It is risky in and of itself and students may recoil and with good reason. Why? Because we are changing the rules to the game while they are playing it. In the end, the creative and cognitive benefits of learning in a risk-ready environment are worth the time, effort, and chance.

One of the key benefits of slowing down the learning process is that it honors the zig-zag nature of deep, meaningful learning. In order to truly learn something and then leverage that knowledge for a creative breakthrough, we must provide the necessary time for iteration and incubation. The worries that surround this process include concerns about both content coverage and—specifically about a project-based approach—that it just takes too long and is too messy. However, creativity experts tell us that those detours and zig-zags are the very point. Purposeful "mind-wondering"[3] and what-iffing have incredible learning benefits. According to Burkus,

> When presented with complicated problems, the mind can often get stuck, finding itself tracing back through certain pathways of thinking again and again. When you work on a problem continuously, you can become fixated on previous solutions. You will just keep thinking of the same uses for that piece of paper instead of new possibilities. Taking a break from the problem and focusing on something else entirely gives the mind some time to release its fixation on the same solutions and let the old pathways fade from memory. Then, when you return to the original problem, your mind is more open to new possibilities.
>
> (p. 25)

In a risk-ready environment students don't have to be right, right now. Instead, they are afforded the chance let ideas, concepts, problems, and projects to simmer and marinate in order to explore ideas deeply and make creative connections. One of the best ways to achieve a balance between the speed of content coverage in K12 classrooms and a creative project approach is what we call S-PBL or Spaced-Project Based Learning.

With S-PBL, we are intentionally acknowledging and leaning into the lack of time needed to dive deeply into topics and combating this time constraint by spacing out our projects *over time*. The consensus from cognitive science is clear: spacing out our practice *works* when it comes to learning.[4] Spacing is one of the best ways to make learning stick; meanwhile, spacing is also one of the best ways to make novel connections. Thus, S-PBL affords time we thought we didn't have, well spent.

S-PBL projects can last a week, a few weeks, a few months, or even an entire school year. Schools such as High Tech High leverage large scaled, spaced projects throughout the year.

Schools we work with that challenge students with end-of-year capstone projects are worth highlighting as well. One magnet school, introduced in Chapter 1, has a senior capstone or thesis project that begins in August and is publicly defended and presented in April. Students work independently as well as alongside teammates and faculty and community mentors on and off throughout the school year to complete the project in a signature way. One STEM team of students asked: What if we could create a new type of body armor for police officers that is more breathable and flexible? This team of students generated their own what-if question fueled by a real-world problem they wanted to solve. And the school provided them with a learning environment to actively lean into the unknown and zig-zag throughout the school year while also covering core content as they took much needed breaks from their daunting project. According to Burkus, creative people willingly take breaks and work on other projects to allow for incubation.[5]

However, not every S-PBL project is formalized like a year-long capstone or thesis project. Another way to leverage S-PBL is through what we call *projects on background*. These are not the *hands-on minds-off* activities that Wiggins and McTighe[6] warn against. These projects are both content-linked as well as crowd-sourced from students and are started, stopped, and resumed in organized spurts throughout a grading period, across a semester, or again across a school year. These projects are often for no credit and are challenge tasks waiting for students to step up and add their signatures. In STEM, for example, a student may ask the class: What if we had an automatic pizza cutting device that could help make more precise and faster cuts? The creative teacher would welcome such a project and establish the necessary low floor of knowledge and materials so that all students could play. In an ELA class, a project on background could be a co-created story built across time where students each add, revise, and reorganize a poem or short story tied to the core content under study. Take for example the case of Kevin's daughter who reorganized a famous poem in a unique way to play with her knowledge and apply it to a new and unique context (Figure 4.1).

Twas the night before Thanksgiving, and all through the house
Not a creature was stirring except for a mouse,
He was lost in a hallway, and scared half to death.
How twitchy his tail, and how squeaky his breath.
He'd run through the door, from his dark attic home,
It had shut right behind him, leaving him to roam.
Now he spied a staircase and started to descend,
Hoping at the bottom he'd find a mouse-friend.
When he reached the last step and found no little mice,
He instead followed the smell of something quite nice.
In a bedroom, he found on the wooden floor,
A string of green lettuce, then two pieces more.
Then up a bedpost he started to creep.
At the top he saw two people laying fast asleep.
The person closest gave him no fear,
So the little mouse scurried over and sniffed at her ear.
Before he could hide, she opened her eyes
And, at the sight of him, screamed in surprise.
As soon as that happened he scampered away
Desperately hoping to be home before day.
When he reached the upstairs he saw a child open the attic door,
He scrambled in stealthily safe once more.
Then he smelled something delicious in small box open wide
When he got in and nibbled it, he was shut up inside.
Twas the night before Thanksgiving and all through the house
Not a creature was stirring, not even a mouse.

- Audrey Krahenbuhl
- 6th Grade, Homeschool Work

FIGURE 4.1

In a social studies class, students could participate in a *Presidents Project*. This project challenges students to volunteer to create a short profile of a president that can then be collected into volume that is shared later in the year. By the end, a profile of each president—past and present—is ready to be showcased and celebrated by the entire class. The exciting part is to see how the tinkering process unfolds and to track the solo and team attempts that start, fizzle, and restart again across time. With these challenging projects constantly lingering in students minds, they can see how real creative work works: messy, non-linear, collaborative, and time-intensive.

Content coverage and time constraints are real but also force us to be creative too. If time is still a concern, reflect alone and with your team about how much time can be dedicated to projects and start small. Perhaps every other Thursday in APUSH (Advanced Placement United States History) is considered "project day." Maybe a two-week study on story structure in third grade could interleave core content standards with an *Itty Bitty Book* project on Wednesdays and Fridays to allow students to test out their knowledge in a signature way. Lando's daughter completed this very project focused on Heroes and Villains and created a story called *Super Donut vs. The Crueller*. The benefits of slowing down, as best we can given our content and context, are undeniable as long as we walk alongside students to ensure the project and creative outputs interlock with the core content under study. Keep in mind the recipe for creativity from Chapter 1: it's original, useful, and useful in the context at hand.

Step 2—Leaning into Failure

Failure is more than just a part of the creative process; it is *instrumental* to the process. Convincing ourselves and our students of this tested and proven truth is no small feat. In a culture of speed where students too often need to be right right now, pushing back against perfectionism is daunting indeed. Agarwal and Bain, authors of *Powerful Teaching*, have proven that this isn't just about creativity; it's about the science of learning as a whole: "How often do we give our students the opportunity to make mistakes, and importantly, how often do we *encourage* them to make mistakes?"[7] In a risk-ready environment, we welcome failures and mistakes and leverage them *for* learning; we strive to help students build a failure tolerance that allows them to build confidence, which makes them more apt and ready to take more risks.

One of the best ways to start the failure *for* learning conversation is to make it a key element of the classroom culture.

Agarwal and Bain, for example, post wall signs that embody the mindsets about learning they want to support and see in action:

- ◆ We all need time to think and learn.
- ◆ It's okay to make mistakes. That's the way we learn.
- ◆ We can do more and learn more when we are willing to take a risk.[8]

These empowering statements are born out of a need to help students understand fundamental truths about how humans learn, but they are also aligned with what we know about the zig-zag nature of the creative process. Here are signs we would add to the walls:

- ◆ We all have creative capacity.
- ◆ We are all tinkerers.
- ◆ Creativity is a team sport.

However, it will take more than wall signs to ensure that students buy-in and believe it. We need modeling that inspires action. Daniel Willingham, author of *Why Students Don't Like School*, provides this advice:

> Try to create a classroom atmosphere in which failure, while not desirable, is neither embarrassing nor wholly negative. Failure means you're about to learn something. You're going to find out that there's something you didn't understand or didn't know how to do. Most important, *model* this attitude for your students. When you fail—and who doesn't?—let them see you take a positive, learning attitude.[9]

This is the embodiment of a risk-ready environment because it is all-inclusive and not just teachers setting expectations for creative thinking, tinkering, and risk-taking but also taking action themselves. From cognitive scientists such as Willingham to children's authors such as Willems, a key step to leaning into failure clearly begins with us.

While modeling this failure positivity themselves, Willingham further argues that teachers should intentionally reveal how hard scientists, authors, innovators, and creators had to work to become what we call signature thinkers.[10] Stuart Firestein, author of *Failure: Why Science is So Successful*, likewise notes how important it is to tell the stories of scientific breakthroughs and the compounding failures required to discover a new truth. The vexing swing of a pendulum, as he recounts, included a *"two-century*-long" record of failures. He states further: "Every fact in science was hard won and has a trail of failures behind it. These failures shouldn't be hidden; they should be featured."[11] Echoing this, Kevin encourages his doctoral candidates who aim to become researchers to absorb every fact and *doubt* every interpretation. Our interpretations are laden with assumptions and often do fail, but through testing and pursuit of what is true we can leverage failure towards success. Without highlighting and celebrating the need for failure in order to innovate, students may see the wall signs but fall back to the longstanding myths that certain people are just born smart and creative and they aren't among the lucky ones.

A key strategy to help students begin to celebrate and showcase their own missteps and errors is to leverage the power of *failure indices*, which are mental bookmarks of failed attempts to solve a problem. Keeping a written or digital journal of these bookmark moments can make recording and sharing failures a normal part of the creative classroom. Prince, Thomas Edison, Leonardo da Vinci, and Judy Blume kept a journal or notebook full of what-ifs and ideas that didn't quite fit—yet. Sawyer provides this advice:

> Keep a notebook, sketchbook, iPad, or voice memo recorder with you at all times, and write down, draw, or record anything you notice that interests you. This kind of notebook, whether paper or digital, is sometimes called a "seed file" because it contains seeds that might one day grow into successful creativity. Use your notebook to keep all of the ideas that seem somehow to have potential, even though you don't yet know exactly how.[12]

Once students learn about how signature thinkers from all fields use failure indices, we can help start the process in the classroom by modeling it ourselves. When we model this for students, we show them the built-in brilliance of bad ideas. In a STEM class, share half-formed what ifs for a new invention or a rough prototype assembled during lunch that day. In an ELA class, share a list of what-ifs for a short story and solicit help from students about which ideas to pursue. In a social studies class, share a list of historical figures to spend a week with on a deserted island or to invite to a dinner party. When students feel comfortable, have them select a way to store their failure indices, whether a physical notebook or on a digital device. Invite students to name the process such as a *thought vault* or an *what-if warehouse*. This provides a chance at ownership in the process while also making it engaging and free from the embarrassment that comes from in-process, unformed ideation. This process does involve risk, but Sawyer reminds us that "if you're never failing, you're never storing failure indices, and that probably means you're playing it too safe."[13]

Step 3—Curating our Policies and Procedures for Creativity

Failure can be the creative thinker's best friend and ally. Helping students believe in the mindset of a risk-ready environment while building a failure tolerance through consistent what-ifs and risks takes time. With the power of failure as a creative learning tool at the forefront of our learning environment, it is imperative that we match the mindset to our classroom policies and procedures.

The research from across domains and discipline is clear that deep learning and creative breakthroughs take time; meanwhile, teachers in K12 schools have never been under more pressure to cover more. Firestein calls this "the tyranny of coverage."[14] This paradox can be addressed with a simple mindset shift: *the due date window*. The due date window approach not only

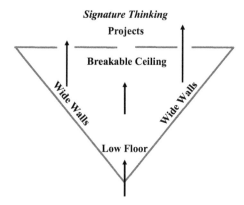

FIGURE 4.2

echoes real-world work but also pairs seamlessly with our S-PBL approach to signature thinking. Remember that our project model, inspired by Resnick, has three key elements (Figure 4.2).

When teachers are launching a signature thinking project, it is crucial to establish the *low floor* so that every student can play our game. This could include providing a guided demonstration, a knowledge-rich opening lecture, a keystone reading, or an excerpt from a documentary. With the low floor established, we establish simultaneous loose and tight constraints upon the project or problem at hand so that students can zig-zag while also staying within the ballpark of the game. One of the most entrenched myths about creativity, according to Burkus, is that we must be free of boundaries and constraints when engaging in creative work or thought. On the contrary, "creativity loves constraints."[15] If we remember how important knowledge is to creative thinking, we know that thinking outside the box isn't always helpful. First, we must *know* the box in order to *break* the box and smash the ceilings we build for students. Without the box, we too often see students drift into another orbit all together, which is how creativity becomes a frivolous fad unworthy of the precious and limited time we have with students.

Innovators and artists who have repeatedly challenged or even broken the box can dismiss deadlines and structure with more ease. While this may be more apt for a professional with a record of signature victories, our students in search of *little-c* wins need limits. Instead of providing no structure and feeding

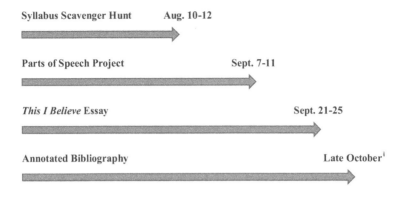

Syllabus Scavenger Hunt   Aug. 10-12

Parts of Speech Project   Sept. 7-11

This I Believe Essay   Sept. 21-25

Annotated Bibliography   Late October[i]

ELA example of S-PBL

FIGURE 4.3

the myth, the due date window approach provides helpful constraints that feed creative thinking and breakthroughs and promote an environment in which we actually see that flexibility is afforded to learners. Figure 4.3 is an example for an eighth grade ELA class practicing the due date window approach to S-PBL. Notice that each project, whether short or long term, has a bandwidth of time for completion, not just *allowing* students to zig-zag within the window but *encouraging* students to think, tinker, pursue a tangent or detour, make errors, and self-correct.

Another example links back to the senior capstone or thesis project mentioned above, which has a window from August to April. The students designing the body armor were under tremendous constraints. With limited resources and funds, they had to get creative and ask *what if?* They procured old vests in order to build prototypes. They interviewed military and law enforcement officers about feasibility and fit. All of this would have been out of reach if the project was due in a month or even two months. In the end, their product was actually safely tested with the guidance of local law enforcement officials who served as community mentors, a signature requirement for this project at the school. This project both needed and deserved the wide walls and lengthy window for it to come to fruition. The *right* constraints were placed upon them, and they were proud to show off their crude yet creative vest that April at the senior expo.

Further, the due date window accepts and promotes the notion that not all students learn at the same pace and aren't ready to take risks all at the same time. The windows also pushback against toxic assessment practices—the wrong kind of constraints—such as grade penalties for late work or partial credit for re-attempting work. The windows, instead, provide time for students to tinker, dabble, and seek feedback from both the teacher and peers. One of the best strategies to tip the scale and make this work is to invite students to help set the due date window parameters and become insiders in the creation of the helpful constraints. Constraints are not only helpful for creative breakthroughs but are also *necessary*. As Sawyer says, "They just have to be the *right* constraints."[16] When students are invited to discuss and debate the constraints, alongside the teacher and their peers, the risk-ready environment begins to solidify into a palpable reality instead of a mere mindset.

Finally, we ask teachers to reflect upon this question: What policies and procedures within our learning environment *prohibit*, *permit*, or *promote* incubation, what-iffing, tinkering, and reflection? In order to make signature thinking the norm, we need policies and procedures that honor the zig-zag and allow students to strike out so that they can build their failure indices. Epstein notes that "Original creators tend to strike out a lot, but they also hit mega grand slams."[17] A risk-ready environment is a creative haven that defends the chance for students to stack their missteps and errors productively so that they can uncover and hone their signatures over time.

Step 4—Tinkering with the Physical Environment

Creative epicenters are built *by design*. From the gardens of Renaissance Florence where sculptors and scientists conversed and shared ideas to the innovative incubators of Silicon Valley, the creative physical space was engineered. Apple and Google, for example, have taken great lengths to ensure that their workspaces are conducive to collaboration, flow, and *aha* moments. Likewise, Burkus notes that WL Gore, the company responsible for Gore-Tex and Elixir guitar strings, sees itself as a "creative marketplace"[18] where the very environment lends itself to fusion and cross-pollination between departments and domains. From furniture arrangements to explicitly designated *what-if* spaces, the physical elements of a risk-ready classroom cannot be overlooked.

First, teachers can begin with a reflection upon the floorplan of their classrooms. Pixar studios and the Apple campuses leverage atriums, conference rooms, and retractable walls to ensure creative thinking and collaboration. With limited resources of schools and teachers, we know that the structural components of classrooms are often unchangeable. However, small tweaks in furniture can help tip the physical space into a creative zone. One of the teachers we work with, for example, places used tennis balls under each chair leg—like many teachers do—but also under each desk and table leg as well. This allows the students to help rebuild or reconfigure the room space at will. In fact, the students practiced so much that a simple call of a formation from the teacher such as "round-table," "pair-up," or "square-up" were the only signals students needed to transform the classroom space in an instant. The teacher was able to leverage, as Sawyer calls it, "guided improvisation"[19] in the moment to welcome the novel detours that arise in a creative classroom. The bonus? The tennis balls provide minimal noise during the transitions.

Second, creating a classroom space where students can openly record ideas and what-ifs is critical. As Sawyer notes, "Your work area should be filled with visible evidence of your creative process: your ideas (and your failures!) should be posted on the walls, the shelves, the bulletin board, and the whiteboard."[20] The whiteboard is of particular significance to becoming a signature thinker. If the classroom already has a large whiteboard, ensure that the board is clean and openly accessible to all students at all times. If possible, hang additional white boards on open walls or use a white sticker adhesive. If wall space is limited, try to procure a rolling or mobile white board for students to record brainstorms and what-ifs. Similar to being able to reconfigure the seating instantly, we want students to swarm the boards when a creative opening arises. Finally, individual white boards or table-top white boards can be another affordable approach, and *Miro* provides a free online white-boarding tool as well. The bottom line is that we want students thinking, iterating, collaborating, and creating in a space that screams *what-if and maybe*. This type of environmental signal lets students know that our first ideas are just that: a small foothold to launch a wealth of what-ifs that can be filed away, fused, and used for creative solutions to novel problems and projects. Make sure to capture the many iterations of ideas and sketches from students as they tinker on the boards. Some teachers we work with use a school-issued iPad to create a digital archive of student ideas and other teachers—often those working with secondary students—encourage students to use a device of their own to house their ideas. No matter the method, we want to use the ABC approach: *Always Be Capturing*. This allows the classroom community to further buy into the notion of storing all ideas, no matter how wild, into our failure indices.

Third, we must ask ourselves what space within our class-rooms we are willing to fully relinquish to creative work. This is reflective of R and D labs and the test kitchens of the real world where the environment is replete with raw materials and openly accessible to all students at all times. In a STEM class, for example, we may have a corner of the room stacked with raw materials for a 3D printer or other projects. In an ELA class, we may have a bank of books, magazines, spiral notebooks, and sticky notes at the ready. In a social studies class, we may have a collection of blank materials for sketching, timeline building, and map making. Instead of these creative spaces being open outside the core class time, as we often see in clubs and after-school activities, we make time and space for this during the regular school day. In these freewheeling creative spaces, what-ifs and maybes are tinkered with and tested. This is where projects on background can be started, stopped, and started again at will. Moreover, these spaces beckon the "chance encounter" where students who normally don't chat or team up can bump into each other and tinker together. Even without the robust resources of Pixar and Apple, our classroom environments can share the same creative spirit Steve Jobs believed in.[21] These dedicated creative spaces, coupled with the flex space mentioned above with classroom furniture and whiteboards, remind students at every turn that the physical layout of the classroom begs them to take a risk and ask what if.

The fourth and final tip for a creative physical space is to invite students to add their signatures to the physical space. This could range from students dedicating a certain whiteboard space or bulletin board to a certain topic or theme such as Haiku Thursday for an ELA class, a quote bank from impactful historical figures in a social studies class, or a wall dedicated to failed prototypes from successful innovators and entrepreneurs in a STEM class. In Keri Carter's eighth grade ELA class, students were invited to find alternative writing spaces within the classroom that made them feel comfortable *and* focused during journal time. One student laid on the floor while another found an unlikely writing nook under Keri's desk. When students are active owners of the creative space, we send signals that their voices matter, are taken seriously, and are safe in the creative haven we have co-constructed. While we integrate these tips to alter our physical space to tip towards creativity we also seek to ensure order remains for there is a harmony in the fusion of order and freedom.[22] Applying these ideas to your environment will help students seek harmony out of the wicked problems we encounter and promote learning that is meaningful within those spaces.

Conclusion

The creative process is latently laced with uncertainty, and there are no guarantees when being creative. Students' new ideas might not work or might not as be innovative as they thought. In their book *The Craft of Creativity*, Cronin and Loewenstein note that uncertainty often leads to paralyzing feelings of "confusion, doubt, fear, or even hopelessness" (p. 186). Furthermore, they state that

> uncertainty makes us feel as if there is no point, as if we are being inefficient, as if we are doing something risky, as if we are disrupting our ability to be understood by and coordinate with others, and worse. Who wants more of that in their lives? Consequently, part of the craft of creativity is managing our emotions and maintaining our motivation to continue our stories in the face of uncertainty.
>
> (p. 188)

Thus, we want to engineer an environment that leverages all of these emotions in our favor. Agarwal and Bain "encourage the students to embrace the feeling of not knowing the answer. It is this feeling of not knowing an answer that will help students succeed."[23] We want students to be ready for these feelings by design—through practice and coaching from their trusted teacher and peers.

In our view, all of these challenging emotions channel toward a keyword: *risk*. Risk is an inescapable element of the creative process, and when being creative doesn't pan out—and it often doesn't—we are tempted to wish we had never tried. We wonder if we should have just stayed the course of our normal thinking. Students often experience these same feelings in school—from kindergarten to twelfth grade. In many cases, the speed of our K12 system is both furious and unforgiving, providing little room for the messy, unorthodox nature of the creative process. Beghetto, in his book *Beautiful Risks*, notes that "Doing things differently is at the heart of creativity. But doing things differently is also risky. These risks are particularly pronounced in educational settings because schools and classrooms tend not to be places where thinking and acting differently is always encouraged or rewarded."[24] But what if we designed a classroom that celebrated the differentness, messiness, uncertainty, and the non-linear zig-zag nature of creativity? This is the *risk-ready environment*.

When starting the journey toward a risk-ready environment that helps uncover and develop students' signatures, there are key questions to reflect and then act upon:

- Are your students allowed to try again?
- Do students have to be right, right now, or can they be right eventually—on different timelines?
- Are students actively challenging each other and you?
- Are students encouraged to break the game you've built for them to play?
- Are students collaborating?
- Does your class provide incubation time?
- Is your class a safe haven?
- Are you coaching and mentoring students?
- Are you tinkering alongside students as they tinker and prototype?
- Are your students talking in *what ifs* and *maybes*?

A risk-ready environment intentionally embraces and celebrates the stories of failures within the domain whether science or songwriting. From R and D labs to test kitchens, the environment in which we work must be conducive to creative thinking. With a risk-ready environment in place, students are now ready for the next stage of signature thinking: *the what-if and maybe mindset*.

Notes

1 Hattie, *Visible Learning for Teachers*, p. 129
2 Sawyer, *Zig Zag*, p. 112
3 Burkus, The Myths of Creativity, p. 25
4 See Willingham's *Why Students Don't Like School*; Brown et al.'s *Make it Stick*; Agarwal & Bain's *Powerful Teaching*
5 Burkus, The Myths of Creativity, p. 22
6 Wiggins & McTighe, *Understanding by Design*, p. 16
7 Agarwal & Bain, *Powerful Teaching*, p. 136
8 Agarwal & Bain, *Powerful Teaching*, p. 137

9   Willingham, *Why Students Don't Like School?* pp. 184–185
10   Willingham, *Why Students Don't Like School?* p. 183
11   Firestein, *Failure*, pp. 73–74
12   Sawyer, *Zig Zag*, p. 97
13   Sawyer, *Zig Zag*, p. 220
14   Firestein, *Failure*, p. 78
15   Burkus, The Myths of Creativity, p. 14
16   Sawyer, *Zig Zag*, p. 117
17   Epstein, *Range*, p. 288
18   Burkus, The Myths of Creativity, p. 45
19   Sawyer, *The Creative Classroom*, p. 35
20   Saywer, *Zig Zag*, p. 224
21   Burkus, The Myths of Creativity, p. 144
22   Clark & Jain, *The Liberal Arts Tradition*
23   Agarwal & Bain, *Powerful Teaching*, p. 124
24   Beghetto, *Beautiful Risks*, p. ix

5

The What If and Maybe Mindset

Time and again, the research on creative individuals illustrates that the ability to shift and move between the *inconceivable* to the *conceivable* is a primary habit of mind. Creators and innovators make these moves no matter the field or domain and do it with aplomb. Sally Ride, knowing that girls were too often left out of the STEM conversation, intentionally asked: *What if* we designed science and engineering programs just for girls?[1] Maria Montessori pondered, "*What if* children could learn in a different environment, one driven by harnessing their innate tendencies to dabble, tinker, and play?[2] We wonder, how do these innovators slide so seamlessly from *what is* to *what could be*? These thinkers stay effective and agile because of the deep and broad knowledge they possess. Sally Ride was an astronaut and physicist. Maria Montessori was a physician and educator. This is why in Chapter 3 we began with a strong emphasis on the role of knowledge for cultivating productive creativity. However, it is not knowledge alone that drives understanding. In fact, many of the greatest scientific discoveries of all time resulted from those

DOI: 10.4324/9781003201380-5

who had built a great deal of knowledge but remained *willing* to ask the all-important question of: *What if?*

Albert Einstein, the famed physicist who developed the Theory of Relativity avoided the possibility of "what if" for nearly a decade because of the radical conclusion that his theory posited. Einstein, when he created the Theory of Relativity, was extremely uncomfortable with the implications of his theory because it pointed to something beyond space, beyond matter, and even beyond time itself. He lived in a scientific world that affirmed the universe existed, eternally, in a "steady state." However, his work on relativity led to the paradigm shattering possibility of: "what if the universe is not eternal but it came into being a finite time ago in the past?" At first, Einstein was unwilling to ask this *what if*. Instead, he built in a "fudge factor" (his own words) into his equations to allow for the steady-state model of the universe to be retained even though the evidence did not seem to fit with it.

This worked for about a decade, but Edwin Hubble, using a telescope in Arizona, confirmed predictions of the theory that forced Einstein to welcome the possibility and consider his *what if*. Hubble, for whom the famous space telescope we have today is named after, was another cosmologist examining the origin of the universe, and his observations proved that the universe was expanding. Einstein came to the telescope to see the evidence for himself and later referred to his inclusion of the "fudge factor" as the biggest mistake he ever made.[3] Ironically, the data forced even Einstein to consider, "what if?" even when the implications were radical.

This same reality is true for other areas beyond science, too. The Post-it Note, according to Burkus, was born out of a series of what-ifs strewn across a dozen years of starts and restarts. Spencer Silver, a 3M employee, was working to improve adhesives for the company. Meanwhile, a chemical engineer named Art Fry was searching for a way to effectively mark the pages of his hymnal while in the choir at Silver's church; the bookmarks just kept falling out of the book. Silver and Fry soon teamed up to ask *what-if* and *maybe* and tinkered with a sticky bookmark prototype for years before anyone at 3M took notice. And it was a mere accident that Fry decided to write a note on the sticky bookmark, which then unlocked the true purpose of their invention. The initial *what-if* sparked a string of problems to solve and winding paths for Silver and Fry to explore. As a candid reminder, it took more than a decade for this team to get their product on the shelf. So when we cultivate the *what-if and maybe mindset*, we must also prepare students for the long-haul thinking and tinkering it brings. Yes, when it comes to moving the needle of understanding beyond basic, an essential part of that is influenced by whether a person is, or is unwilling or unable, to reflect on multiple possibilities.

The world is full of checklists and tick boxes. We crave both clean and clear answers to complicated questions and often want those answers *now*. Breakthroughs, however, don't arise cleanly, clearly, or quickly. Instead, breakthroughs begin by leaning into uncertainty, welcoming the messiness of our complicated existence, and daring to ask *what if*? Talking in *what-ifs* and *maybes* is at the core of what we call *Signature Thinking*. By embracing these thinking habits, we acknowledge that sometimes our wants, our feelings, our knowledge, and our energies are in flux. Creative thinkers change their minds all the time, and we want to help teachers help students recognize and harness that as a creative learning tool.

What If and Maybe and the Classroom

Saying what if and/or maybe serves in many ways as an action that necessitates vulnerability. It affirms, to oneself and the audience, that you don't have the right answer, or perhaps more unnervingly, that there may not be a single right answer. Either way, this willful acknowledgement of uncertainty is humbling. This is, however, a necessary catalyst for creative thinking.

At the very core of learning to think creatively, and in ways that tip towards deeper learning, is the challenge of asking quality questions. Robinson notes that "students [need to be] encouraged to ask questions, to look for alternative and unusual answers, and to exercise their powers of creativity and imagination."[4] In fact, the literature surrounding creativity is littered with reflections on the importance of asking good questions, but there is neither clear nor consistent guidance on how to teach this.[5] Learning to ask good questions occurs readily through the what if and maybe mindset. Furthermore, it encourages learners to become *problem finders*.[6] Indeed, Csikszentmihalyi points out the need to become a *problem finder* before a *problem solver*.

We begin with widening the walls of our current lessons, units, and projects. This means that we embrace the notion that students need the autonomy to choose how they want to pursue their learning and problem solving. This is a messy process riddled with uncertainties, which is why many of us shy away from it. However, uncertainty is a fundamental element of being creative. Matthew Cronin and Jeffrey Loewenstein note in their book *The Craft of Creativity* that uncertainty is "unavoidable and pervasive in the creative process."[7] In a classic text on leisure and the contemplative life of learners, Joseph Pieper explains that the fusion of positive and negative and the fusion of ignorance on the path to wisdom helps us to find that wonder has the same structure of hope.[8] Our consistent commitment to cultivating a sense of wonder in our students begins with the what if and maybe mindset. And, as the designers of their learning experience, we must lean into the uncertainty that accompanies creativity in order to ignite students' passions and tip them towards hope.

One of the best approaches is to practice the *what if and maybe mindset* ourselves. We ask: What if we could have students team up to explore who they are as a generation and present the results to the community? What if students could learn history through a meeting of the minds? What if we could have students build their own statistical models to make sense of health care trends and patterns? What if we could—as John Hunter[9] did—have students play a *World Peace* game to understand the complexities of our lives? We won't know exactly how these *what ifs?* will turn out, but we lean into the uncertainty anyway.

The goal is to reclaim passion through an all-inclusive embrace of the messy, non-linear nature of creative thinking so that the students and teachers alike develop the persistence to keep *zig zagging* through the games we've built for them to play. If we can tap into students' passions through leaning into uncertainty and asking *what if?*, we will have a direct pipeline to student engagement, autonomy, and motivation. With the monotony of school banished from our classrooms, students will have the drive and determination to find their signatures.

The Power of Possibility

In addition to the ways that what if and maybe can inform how we design lessons, design our environment, how we encourage students to engage in lessons, and how we, ourselves, engage with ideas, there are more benefits that come from thinking in such terms. The essence of asking what if or considering maybe is *imagination*. We want to encourage students to not simply take in information and absorb it as is. We want them to actively interact with that information. We want them *riffing* and *spitballing* as they engage and make sense of content. Absorbing the best information available and then seeking to consider the implications it offers in other contexts leads students naturally to *elaboration*. And research has consistently demonstrated that when learners elaborate upon what they learn, it leads to better long-term retention of that knowledge and, consequently, better capacity to use that knowledge.[10] Through asking questions such as "what if" and considering "maybe," subsequent retention of knowledge is greatly enhanced in learners.[11] This is thought to be one of the most powerful ways to enhance our memory of information and it is also recognized to work across age levels, so it's relevant in any learning context.[12]

As educators, we make it our commitment to harness the power of possibility and empower our students by considering what is possible based upon what we know. This will lead to a risk-ready environment where curiosity, imagination, and sincere engagement with ideas we're learning about are the norm, not the exception. Classrooms that are framed around an unending battle between knowing and wondering—between knowledge and imagination—between what is real and what is possible—are tipped towards *signature thinking*. This is the distinct marker of a *signature thinking* classroom: while knowledge is prioritized, it is not for its own sake, but for the possibilities it affords. The building of our knowledge enhances our awareness of what we know and how much we don't know, it focuses and improves the quality of questions that we ask, and it helps us imagine possibilities. And all of this can be won by leaning into two ideas: encouraging students to consider "what if" and "maybe." Let's look at some specific strategies that we can use to cultivate this what if and maybe mindset in the classroom.

Cultivating a What If and Maybe Mindset

In this section we will present seven different strategies to help you and your students cultivate a what if and maybe mindset. Each strategy will be discussed and provide a specific example of what it could look like in action. We've chosen these because they're all scalable and we'll have to consider: What if I put this to work in my context? Maybe it could look like this? Or That?

Break the Game

This strategy is foundational to helping students get comfortable with talking in what ifs and maybes. With this strategy, we intentionally ask students to challenge the very knowledge we've taught them about a subject, genre, or discipline. In our workshops with teachers, we employ this strategy within the first minutes by passing out random cards that say *vampires*, *zombies*, *alien invasion*, or *haunted house*. Whatever card teachers receive, they must think of as many ways to tell that type of story that we've never seen before. The results are often wild and won't quite work, but there's often one idea on each card that makes us reconsider the genre altogether. For example, one teacher said, "What if the vampires give instead of take blood? Maybe they are trying to save us somehow?"

We see teachers conjure up, in only two minutes, ideas like this all the time. We simply need to apply exercises like this in our own classrooms to make this the new normal. Give students two minutes to ponder, riff, and spitball:

- ♦ What if we piloted pop-up grocery trucks to help alleviate neighborhood food deserts?
- ♦ Maybe we could alter the supply chain in a way that's both more productive and less harmful to the environment?
- ♦ What if we implemented renegotiable GPA where students could loop back to prior grades and demonstrate new levels of learning?
- ♦ What if we ran a different statistical model to see if we can find root causes of injuries among professional athletes?
- ♦ What if we built our own textbook?
- ♦ What if we answered the Common App essay with a poem?
- ♦ What if we told the story from the perspective of the Miss Trunchbull?

What seems silly at first, when some receive their cards with *vampires* or *alien invasion*, actually provides a chance to retrieve knowledge and deliberately flip or reverse key ideas to see *what could be* instead. Rear Admiral Grace Hopper used her deep and technical knowledge of computer coding to ask a Big C flipped question: *What if* we could develop a coding language in English rather than numbers? COBOL, the widely used computing language, was born.[13] Further, Sawyer writes about the power of reversing the question and retells the story of Henry Ford's automotive breakthrough. Originally, his idea was focused on waves of specialized teams taking turns working on a stationary car. By reversing the question, Ford asked: *What if* we could bring the *car* to the *teams*? And the assembly line was born.[14]

Give Students Feedback on Quality of Questions Asked

One simple way we can start to operationalize this is to revisit how we look at classroom participation or engagement. Whether or not we assign any grade for this necessary part of being a student is not the focus here. What we are zeroing in on is two-fold. First, we demand that students engage in our classrooms in a way that considers myriad possibilities. Students struggle to excel if they are not curious about what they are learning, so lean into it; do not accept them leaving the class without ever wondering about the topics under study. Second, provide consistent feedback to students that speaks to them directly about the quality of questions they are asking. This feedback serves an important formative function: it tells learners that we care about the fact that they ask questions and that they ask quality questions.

Below is an illustration of a form Kevin uses with his students to provide weekly feedback related to participation in class (Figure 5.1). You will notice that it is notably weighted in favor of the quality of questions that students ask. One additional note to share is that we don't recommend using participation for grades unless we have an outcome associated directly with mastery of one of the features provided. When used in Kevin's class, this is used formatively and for the purpose of encouraging students to think deeply about questions and possibilities as they relate to topics we are examining and do not go into the gradebook immediately. Additionally, this form is used in college classrooms and ought to be adjusted for specific contexts, but it helps provide a model for quality questioning and sending clear signals that what-iffing is not an option but is a key strategy for how we can tip students towards thinking in what ifs and maybes.

Through a consistent delivery of feedback that tips students towards asking questions and towards thinking in what if and maybe, we'll train them to ask both precise and extended questions. In doing so, we also help students become problem finders who help steer where we *could go*.

RUBRIC FOR EVALUATING SESSION PARTICIPATION

Performance Elementsor Criteria	Inadequate	Basic, Below Expectations	Proficient, Meets Expectations	Exemplary, Displays Leadership	Score
Quality of Questions Asked	Does not ask questions or only ones that are off-topic and/or insignificant (0)	Asks questions that are relevant to the course but basic (3)	Asks quality questions relevant to the topic and at both basic and	Asks strong questions that positively contribute to the class overall by considering implications, extending thoughts, pose relevant what if and maybe ideas, etc. (5)	
Relevance of Contribution to Discussion Topic	Contributions, when made, are off-topic or distract class from discussion (0)	Contributions are relevant mostly, although sometimes off-topic (1)	Contributions are relevant and promote deeper analysis of the topic (2)		
Preparation	Student is not adequately prepared. Has not read required material or fully completed the assignment(s) in advance of class (0)		Student has read and thought about the material in advance of the class. Assignments are completed and notes and materials are brought to class. (1)		
Level of Engagement with Collective Discussion	Student never contributes to class discussion; fails to respond to direct questions. Is disengaged (0)	Few contributions to class discussion. Seldom volunteers but responds to direct questions. (1)	Proactively contributes to class discussion, asking questions and responds to direct questions. (2)		

** Parentheses indicate total possible points awarded from each section **

FIGURE 5.1

Create a Possibility Journal

Ask each student to keep a journal where they store their thoughts about the class and consider, frequently, what if and maybe. Prince was known to take his *purple notebook* everywhere he went to capture the tendrils of songs or even what-ifs for an entire album. For our students, this could simply be a section at the front of their three-ring binder that is visited and revisited weekly for just a few minutes. In fact, we'd recommend doing so as part of an ongoing review where students can zig and zag between old and new what-ifs and maybes. As we close out one week, or open up the next, invite students to reenter their "What If/Maybe Possibility" section. Give them a few minutes of silent contemplation on what we have been studying and then invite them to jot down some thoughts. Encourage them to use the prongs of "what if" and "maybe." We can also provide a template that includes these as headers including space underneath each where students will use it as a starter for their extended thinking about what they have been learning in class and imagining what is possible and making novel connections between past and present wonderings.

Another way we can use this "What If/Maybe Journal" or Possibility Journal is to leverage student interest, and get additional, consistent formative data on what and where they are thinking. This journal operates as its own *wide walls* where we can quickly check in on their thinking and leverage it for both correction and extension. When their what ifs are leaning towards a potential line of erroneous or otherwise negative thinking, we can intervene while it's emergent and prepare a lesson to help redirect them. When their what if's point us in a direction we had not planned *but that could be fruitful*, we can capitalize on these moments and show them that they are truly thinking partners with us who are invited, as an apprentice, on this learning journey, not just as a passive recipient of our knowledge and leadership.

Challenge Students to Theorize

The core of what drives scientific discovery are theories that explain reality. The theories we've likely heard of are composite fusions of previous discoveries and illustrate the ultimate examples of what Theresa Amabile calls Big C creativity.[15] However, all of these began with very basic, little C creativity considerations of what is possible. Whether it was Galen or Galileo, breakthroughs begin with what ifs and maybes. Thus, encourage students to think about what they are learning and form theories to explain them.

In science, a good theory typically consists of several important characteristics. These include a general explanation of something that is descriptive and can be applied, and it ought to be falsifiable, meaning that it is not assumed true and used to explain away all data it encounters. They should also have internal consistency and be open to measurement and evaluation. Using these characteristics, we can help students adjust their emerging theories to account for more of these elements in their refined theories. One example comes from an elementary classroom. Imagine encouraging students to think, early in the year, about what things *change*. As the class considers what things change, it is likely that at some point they'll stumble onto the idea that *they* will change. At this point, we might offer an opportunity for students to theorize how they will change this year. Then they could be challenged to attempt to explain how those changes might occur using drawings, words, or digital media. Next, they can even test out their theories by revisiting them later in the year or developing predictions that could be tested soon.

Theorizing also supports calculated risk-taking and promotes out-of-the-box thinking while simultaneously respecting the deep and established knowledge within the box. Inviting students on the path of developing theories will also open them up to seeing how hard it is to be right all the time, and that will invite a healthy conversation for students about how scientists are not right all the time, either. In fact, they're wrong *a lot*. Firestein notes that science is a "process replete with wrong turns, cul-de-sacs, and circularities in which facts are declared right, then wrong, and then sometimes right again."[16] The words *what if* and *maybe* paved the road toward discovery, all in the face of uncertainty. Just like the experts, we acknowledge from the start that we might be wrong, but we do so with generations of good company.

In developing their theories, students will generate basic ideas that attempt to explain patterns they are seeing. They will be using what if and maybe at the core of their efforts to generate these, and it will lead to predictions that we might even be able to capitalize on to extend learning. If students come up with a tentative theory that has a prediction associated with it, encourage them to test it out. Challenging students to theorize invites them to engage in little C creativity on purpose in the same way that famed scientists do with big C creativity.

Leverage What If and Maybe in Feedback to Students

Rather than simply recording a score or marking a rubric indicating what a student did well or did not do well on, help guide students towards growth. Ronald Beghetto suggests that "preferencing your feedback with 'what if' . . . can be a powerful way of providing an honest critique to students."[17] Consider the following example from Kevin's former high school government class he taught. Rupert was a student in Kevin's government and politics class.

As an activity to encourage review of past concepts and extending understanding, students were asked to create a "Topic" for a Kids lesson or lesson materials. Each student could pick any topic we had prioritized during our class and was challenged to simplify the important aspects of it so that a third grader could learn it. Rupert chose the federal bureaucracy—not necessarily a favorite topic among students. His initial submission was a sketched, three-picture cartoon he had drawn as an initial prototype for approval and is shown below (Figure 5.2).

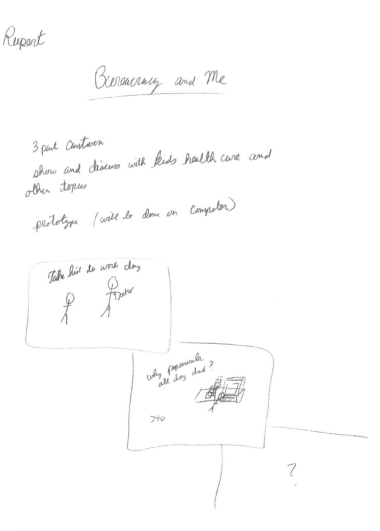

FIGURE 5.2

In reviewing his prototype, Kevin had a quick feedback form with a short checklist on one side and thoughts to consider on the other. What if and maybe are embedded directly into the feedback form as we can see in Figure 5.3.

Government "Topic" for Kids Lesson Activity
Prototype Review Feedback Form

Very Interesting	This Works	Develop More	Criteria	Thoughts to Consider
✓			Topic Addresses Key Content	What if you give it a title that tips them toward your form?
	✓		Relevant & Significant Focus	
	✓		Accuracy of Topic	Maybe you need a bit more then 3 quick cartoons to do this and maybe
	✓		Creative Presentation of Topic	a topic kids know more about then health care?

FIGURE 5.3

Rupert took the feedback to heart and ran with it. He produced a 12-page flipbook and brought in six copies of it so he could have the third graders look at it in groups, and he'd then lead a discussion after. Rather than simply giving a grade on his prototype, or a stamp of approval, the use of what ifs and maybes helped catalyze further thinking and tinkering that led to an improved product—and one that went beyond Kevin's initial conception, too, as it held Rupert's unique signature that broke the ceiling. The figure below (Figure 5.4) provides an image of the cover page of his flipbook for kids. When we had our third grade students visit our classroom, Rupert's book was a hit. Afterwards, he exemplified the what if and maybe mindset as he told me: *maybe* I should have added in some guiding questions? Using what if and maybe consistently in our feedback can help learners think in what ifs and maybes too, encouraging a consistent growth attitude, fueled by possibility.

arcadio / La Prensa

The Bureaucratic Maze

FIGURE 5.4

The Five Whys

The Five Whys process, as outline by Sawyer in his book *Zig Zag*, helps students engage in deep thinking and searching for root causes. Once students pose an intriguing theory or question born from a what if or maybe, they can use the Five Whys process to stretch, push, and pull their thinking in new directions.

Generation Project Example	STEM Senior Thesis Example
Why don't parents and teachers respect our generation? (because they see us as lazy and obsessed with our phones)	Why does the body armor not work? (because the design limits movement too much)
Why do they see us that way? (because they see us online or with our phones so much)	Why does the design limit movement too much? (because we failed to test the prototype on a real law enforcement officer to get user feedback)
Why do they see us online or with our phones so much? (because that's the main way we live our lives and communicate)	Why did we fail to get user feedback? (because we ran out of time and cut the user test from our timeline)
Why is this the main way we live our lives and communicate? (because the world has changed since our parents were teenagers and this is the new normal)	Why did we run out of time? (because we focused too much on the color designs and marketing materials)
How can we change parents' and teachers' mindsets of our generation as more than lazy and obsessed with our phones?	How can we improve our planning, focus, and timeline challenges we encountered before the next due date?

When students use the Five Whys protocol, they stretch their problem or question until they get a "powerful new formulation of the problem"[18] and can continue the what-if and maybe mindset even further.

Playing with the Past

One more activity that we encourage to include in classrooms to help develop the what if and maybe mindset is a healthy juxtaposition of reality with possibility. We call this *Playing With the Past*, which is not limited to history and social studies because all subjects and domains have important stories and timelines to understand. Begin by studying a topic and getting an accurate understanding of what it is. Let's take a historical example. Suppose we are second grade teachers and our students are learning about their state's history. There is a real history to your state that includes basic, immutable facts, such as when it joined the Union, what form of government it has by constitution, and how its laws will be passed. Whatever the learning goals are, derived from your state standards, form the *low floor* basis of *what is*.

But what if after we built the low floor we paused and asked our students: *what if* things happened differently? Maybe our state would be different. How do we think that might have occurred? What impact would that have had? Leveraging this type of playing with the past is a fantastic way to help students learn to interpret events in context and not from their viewpoint, which is a key facet of historical understanding.[19] Using this short line of questioning could lead into a short activity where students offer some of their own thoughts about what might have been or what could be and open up the gateway to critical thinking. After imagining possible alternatives, we close out with a compare and contrast of reality with possibility: *what is* versus *what could be*. And that might help us—and our students—think about what some of the differences are, *why* they are different, and *what* they might be able to do about them—or not.

This activity is flexible across disciplines. What if this battle had went a different way? What if a scientific discovery had been made 100 years earlier, or later, and on a different continent? This strategy works for the arts too. Marvel's TV series *What if...?* intentionally inverts or undoes major moments from the comics and films to see how the alternate outcome would play out. This activity is also scalable from elementary grades onward. In short, *Playing With the Past* invites students to use their foundational knowledge to explicitly ask *what could* or *would have been* in order to dive deeper into their knowledge of key facts, figures, dates, and discoveries.

Conclusion

The what if and maybe mindset is a crucial precursor to successful tinkering and prototyping. These what ifs and maybes are often tested within the wide walls afforded by signature thinking teachers through tinkering and the building of prototypes. However, what if and maybe is not a one-and-done exercise; it is an all-the-time idea enterprise. Asking what if and considering maybe occurs throughout the entire signature thinking process in cyclical, non-linear ways. In so doing, it becomes a characteristic, perhaps defining feature, of a signature thinking classroom. This is because it is a mindset. We want to help our students develop a habit of mind to think in terms of what if and maybe so that they see possibilities and seek out problems and lean into them in search of deeper learning.

When teachers and their students think and talk if *what ifs* and *maybes* they start to realize that they don't have to be right, right now. They recognize that getting things right is important, but it isn't an important *first* step, and that many missteps will soon follow in the quest to get it right. We are empowering students to think in terms of possibilities. Creative people know that the seeds of something special are born out of asking *what if* and embracing the uncertainty of *maybes*. Perhaps the most brilliant aspect of "What if" and "Maybe" is that it invites us to participate. What if we asked ourselves to share with a colleague one way we could help students think in terms of possibilities, in terms of maybe, and considering what if? I'm betting we already have an idea to share. Maybe we should?

Notes

1   Clinton & Boiger, *She Persisted*
2   Beevor & Green, *Amazing Women*, p. 52
3   https://www.nytimes.com/1998/05/26/science/essay-a-famous-einstein-fudge-returns-to-haunt-cosmology.html
4   Robinson & Aronica, *Creative Schools*, pp. 36–37
5   See Wagner's *Global Achievement Gap* and *Creating Innovators*; Sawyer's *Zig Zag*; Beghetto's *What If?*
6   Csikszentmihalyi, *Creativity*,
7   Cronin & Loewenstein, *The Craft of Creativity*, p. 186
8   Pieper, *Leisure: The Basis of Culture*, p. 117
9   TED, *Teaching with the World Peace Game*, TED Talk.
10 Karpicke et al., "Retrieval-Based Learning"

11 Craik & Tulving, "Depth of Processing and the Retention"
12 Bartsch & Oberauer, "The Effects of Elaboration"
13 https://obamawhitehouse.archives.gov/women-in-stem
14 Sawyer, *Zig Zag*, p. 43
15 Here is a publicly available work from Teresa Amabile exploring "Big C and Little C" creativity: https://www.hbs.edu/ris/Publication%20Files/12-085_eb9ecda0-ec0a-4a32-8747-884303f8b4dd.pdf
16 Firestein, *Failure*, p. 98
17 Beghetto, "Respond Creatively," p. 86
18 Sawyer, *Zig Zag*, p. 46
19 Seixas and Morton, *The Big Six*.

6

Tinkering and Prototyping

Tinkering. Dabbling. Piddling. Fiddling. There are many sound arguments for teaching creative thinking in discipline-specific ways, but these are the crosscutting keywords and habits of mind found in real creative environments across cultures, continents, domains, and history. The scratch track laid down in the recording studio. The new dish born in the test kitchen. The wild model we've never seen built in the R and D lab. All of these creative spaces are fueled by tinkering and prototyping. It is our responsibility to honor these truths and dedicate the time, space, materials, resources, and patience in our own creative classrooms. In *Beautiful Risks*, Beghetto argues that building creative confidence takes time.

> By providing students with multiple opportunities to creatively respond to learning tasks and reflect on those responses, you can support their creative confidence beliefs and help them recognize the value of creative expression.[1]

DOI: 10.4324/9781003201380-6

We can help our students build that incremental confidence through the tinkering and prototyping process. With a risk-ready learning environment in place, one that invites students to ask what-if and talk in maybes, to slow down and embrace failure, we are now ready to unleash the proven power of tinkering and prototyping for creative learning for all students.

Fail Fast and Fail Often

Remember, failure is the creative tinkerer's best friend. Tinkerers are also doers who are unafraid of looking foolish or imperfect. They make quick models and even quicker mistakes in order to jumpstart the zig-zagging process and enter *flow*. From scientists to storytellers, tinkerers willingly generate tons of ideas to solve a problem or to fuel a project and actively let many of the ideas stay filed away. Tinkerers possess the courage to quit and to leave projects unfinished. They don't see them as a waste of time; rather, they view them as helpful or controlled failures that either will help them with another project down the road or for potential to combine ideas once they step away from the project to allow for incubation, which is when surprise revelations often occur. Moreover, Resnick describes the tinkerer perfectly in his book *Lifelong Kindergarten*: "Tinkerers understand how to improvise, adapt, and iterate, so they're never hung up on old plans as new situations arise. Tinkering breeds creativity."[2] The demands of the 21st century are many, but persistence and perseverance are high premium traits sought after by universities, businesses, technological firms, and the military. It is for these reasons, and many more, that we want to help students believe in and see themselves as tinkerers.

To encourage students to fail fast and fail often, start by having students *cast the widest net* possible when approaching a key question, problem, or project. Like we saw in Chapter 3 with the *ballpark* exercise, think of ways to get students asking *what if* so that they can actively generate both good and bad ideas. For example, in Lando's creative writing class, he uses an exercise called *the basket* where students write the title of a potential short story on a slip of paper and place it in a basket. As the basket moves around the room, the students fill it with slips of paper and is quickly brimming with possibilities. Once all students have contributed a title, the slips are shuffled and the basket is sent around the room again so that students can draw a new slip at random. The next step is where we activate the *what-if and maybe mindset* to have students generate as many ideas as possible for a short story that fits their title. Leveraging our whiteboard spaces, our R and D labs, or individual think-spaces at desks, students can unleash every idea they can think of during what we call a *2 minute drill*. This time constraint helps students—especially after this practice becomes the norm—dismiss the need to be *right, right now* and lean into any and all possibilities. In a *risk-ready* environment where students know that our first ideas aren't often our most creative and innovative ideas, they can free themselves from the pressure to perform and to strike gold immediately. Instead, they now have ammunition to send them into the tinkering and prototyping phrase of signature thinking with a creative confidence.

Next, have students tour the room to see the volume of possibilities their peers generated. Have students walk the room with a notepad to record ideas that both excite or catch their attention; students can also mark, circle, or star the boards or charts as well. Open the class for a discussion of ideas or have students volunteer to share their top three ideas. Next, have students work alone and in pairs to *pressure test* the initial ideas generated from casting the widest net. This example is drawn from a creative writing classroom, but the mindset is the same no matter the discipline because we must think hard about which ideas are worthy of pursuit. As Sawyer says, "To be creative, you have to generate boatloads of ideas. To be creative successfully, you have to let most of them sink, because the real genius lies in picking good ideas."[3] Here are some key questions for students to ask themselves, each other, and you:

- ◆ Which ideas have I seen before?
- ◆ Which ideas have potential to work?

- ◆ Which ideas can be combined, if any?
- ◆ Which ideas will help me do something a little bit different?

Winnowing down ideas to the top two to three can be an unnerving process. Students often choose too quickly from a list that's too short and get stuck with an idea or project they aren't excited about—or one that simply isn't feasible for the task at hand or time given. Casting the widest net helps students avoid these pitfalls. With trusted peers to help and a creative teacher walking alongside students, the honing process becomes doable and fun and students can learn to discriminate between ideas that have novel potential and ones that can be stored in the *what-if warehouse* for later use.

The Multiple Benefits of Multiple Modeling

The inklings of signature thinking can be traced back to our own students showing us what we had yet to discover ourselves about the power of creative thinking in the classroom. At Lando's school, he cofounded and codirected an in-house writing lab where students of all ages and backgrounds in Grades 6–12 could visit on their own volition to receive on-demand writing assistance from a trusted peer. The writing lab was popular from the start among students and teachers, but we wanted to find a way to advertise on a larger scale that we indeed existed but also what we did for students. Collaboratively, the students came up with a mission for the writing lab: *Writers helping writers in the right place.* Creating the mission then led to needing a banner of some kind to showcase our slogan and location in the school. One student named Chandler volunteered to work on the banner design, and in only a few days he came to class with *four* different versions for us to see (Figure 6.1).

We were stunned that he took the time to develop multiple mock-ups of the banner on his own and for no credit or points. Lando's obsession with making, tinkering, and building multiple prototypes the new normal was born.

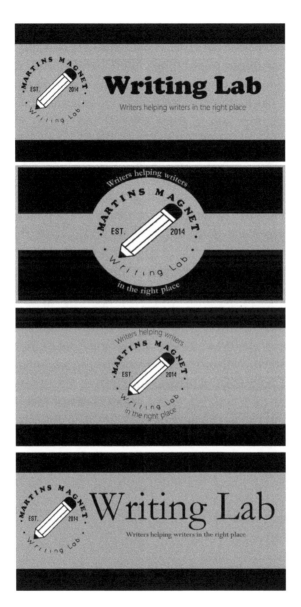

FIGURE 6.1

Chandler's four prototypes are great examples of signature thinking in action. He thought, "What if the banner looked like this?" "What if the logo was positioned like that?" Chandler showed the time, patience, and vulnerability it takes to move multiple what ifs and maybes into the tinkering and prototyping phase of the creative process. When students cast the widest net, thinking of multiple possibilities like Chandler did, they have a reservoir of ideas to draw from to begin the tinkering and prototyping process. No matter the discipline, we can encourage students to move their top two to three *what-ifs and maybes* for a project into reality through building rough sketches or prototypes of each. Indeed, this does mean that students will be spending precious and limited time tinkering with two to three ideas for a project. The benefits are worth the time investment, however. David Epstein, in his book *Range*, warns against our culture of speed and the "pick and stick" approach to sports, majors, and careers that pressure young people to pick quick and specialize sooner rather than later.[4] Too often students are stuck with a project that doesn't speak to their passion but also may not be feasible or achievable. Multiple modeling provides time for students to discover their passion and signature approach to a project or problem while also mirroring the methods of the best creators and innovators in the real world.

We can start small and save time by having students create multiple project proposals, which is an effective and more structured way to move their what-ifs into a more concrete format. Create a quick-to-complete template that captures key information while also providing the wide walls of the project (Figure 6.2).

What is your big idea?
How is this novel _and_ useful?
What is your timeline based on the *Due Date Window* given?
What knowledge must you seek in order to be successful?
What materials will you need?

FIGURE 6.2

Once students have completed a proposal, have them complete one to two more based on the ideas that made the collective cut from their widest net list or ballpark map. The students will now be primed and ready to square each proposal against each other in order to clarify which project they should pursue that is not only novel but actually has the potential to work. This warring proposal process can also be looser, depending on the project, problem, or timeline. For an ELA class, this could be as simple as laying out multiple research questions for a research paper or multiple arguments for a persuasive essay. For a STEM class, this could be rough, hand-drawn sketches for different ways to approach an innovation such as a nighttime running vest or designs for a moon buggy. For a social studies class, this could be debating different ways to illustrate the trends and patterns across wars from different eras. For a business class, this could be bulleted outlines for multiple ways to launch a product or business.

Once students have mock-ups of multiple working models, they can then start the pressure testing phase once more, which allows them to reinter the what-if and maybe cycle. This is where we help students move beyond the excitement of a new idea to testing the feasibility of an idea. This is when *hard fun*[5] occurs. Creativity is sometimes dismissed as mere play, especially in classrooms where high stakes tests are seen as serious business. In the real world, however, creativity is taken quite seriously. Conan O'Brien, while sitting with James Lipton on Inside the Actor's studio, described the creative process and taxing work ethic required to make people laugh. O'Brien described sitting in the writers' room as each team member shared their ideas for a monologue or a sketch. And, surprisingly, there's not much laughter in the room, not because the jokes weren't funny but because of the deathly serious nature of comedy. As the writers would pitch a joke, the team would nod gravely or ruminate stone-faced while dissecting the joke in their minds. Then, someone would say, with a stern countenance: "Yeah. That's really funny." And then the next layer of creative labor begins: the punch-up process. When successful jokes are shared in the writers' room, they then go through the punch-up process where the team tinkers with the jokes to amplify the funniness—to max out its impact on the audience. Ironically, the creative work of comedy is quite serious, and so too for the creative work in the classroom, especially when play is aligned with a specific purpose rooted in students' genuine passions as they also pursue these passions in a safe, collaborative, and risk-ready environment.

So, have students pressure test or punch-up each model. Teach students how Apple engineers find the beauty of glitches in the source code—how the errors lead to improvements. Teach students to find and celebrate the flaw in a prototype. Eventually, they will be excited to uncover an error or pitfall in a design. Have them forecast future problems with each prototype. For an ELA class, this could be having students work in pairs to help foolproof an argumentative essay against crucial counterpoints from the opposing side. With multiple thesis statements or arguments at the ready, students can continue their problem finding habits of mind. This is when students can learn to creatively spin a counterclaim in their own favor through reflecting not only on their own argument but also on what they don't yet know about a subject or problem under study. This process encourages students to read deeper and broader now that they have working prototypes under pressure to discover which innovative argument stands strongest. In a STEM class, students can take multiple models from their sketchpads or even a 3D printer and begin the same process seen in the ELA example of pressure testing to see which model is indeed worthy of pursuit. Have students pair up to crosscheck their innovations against current patents to see if an idea infringes too closely on an existing idea. Further, have students work together to create a ballpark budget of what it will cost to move each prototype to the next phase of production.

Having students work collaboratively to pressure test their ideas and models will help them become, as Sawyer says, the *masters of choosing*.[6] Once students make the tough decision about which model makes the cut, they are ready to continue the tinkering and prototyping process with an idea, blueprint, or physical model that they are not only passionate about but also confident can be achieved given the time and resource constraints they face. Again, a bonus of this process is that students are given time to work up multiple sketches or models before committing to a pathway forward. Too often we see students pushed to pick a topic for a project before they have had a chance to dabble with different ideas and approaches. Pushing back against this culture of speed, once again, is vital to the success of the tinkering and prototyping process. With students working with peers and alongside their teacher, we ensure that creative work is productive and doesn't fall prey to what Wiggins and McTighe call *hands-on, minds-off learning*.

Fusion and Cross-Pollination

The final and most exciting element of multiple modeling is the chance for *fusion*. At the heart of almost all creative break-throughs is the fusion of ideas, approaches, or materials that don't normally belong in the same notebook, room, or bin. According to Tina Seelig, author of *InGenius*, "Being able to connect and combine nonobvious ideas and objects is essential for innovation and a key part of the creative-thinking process."[7] The film *Bone Tomahawk*, for example, brilliantly fuses the tra-ditional western with elements of horror, making for a novel and successful cross-pollination of genres; the signature is now unmistakable. Likewise, Steve Jobs was able to stand at the nexus of the arts and technology to create a host of signature products we had never seen before. With the tinkering and prototyping process at the core of our project-based approach, there are several ways to tip our classrooms toward fusion.

First, we want students to continue their warring of proto-types to see what can be used and fused between them in order to make a newly refined, combined, and novel approach to a project or problem. Essentially, we want to encourage students to become *mad scientists*. The root of this working in a real classroom comes from a standard resume project. High school students in Lando's class, in conjunction with the guidance department, were tasked to create a formal resume with the standard headings, content, fonts, and colors in order to prepare for college applica-tions and entering the workforce. One year, a wave of students began questioning the effectiveness and relevance of the standard business template they were asked to use. With the then unnamed signature thinking mantra in mind of *doing something a little bit different*, they began asking for permission to create a *21st Century Resume* alongside the traditional template. Lando excitedly accepted their suggestion, and students started asking what if, tinkering, and building multiple prototypes. The traditional resumes looked clean and crisp, and yet students now had wild and innovative designs to lay next to their stock and safe designs (Figure 6.3).

NAME
ADDRESS
CITY, STATE, ZIP
(AREA CODE) TELEPHONE
EMAIL ADDRESS

RÉSUMÉ OF QUALIFICATIONS

2018-Present: Senior at

GPA: ACT: SAT: (if taken) Offices Service hours	Clubs Awards Activities Sports

2017-2018: Junior at

Offices Clubs Awards	Activities Sports Service Hours

2016-2017: Sophomore at

Offices Clubs Awards	Activities Sports Service Hours

2015-2016: Freshman at

Offices Clubs Awards	Activities Sports Service Hours

OTHER ACTIVITIES: Mission trips, youth groups, camps, conferences

WORK EXPERIENCE: Tutoring, camp instructor, job, volunteer work

HOBBIES & INTERESTS:

(Fill the page, but keep to one page. Use columns if necessary to keep it to one page. Use plain type. If you choose a border, make it business-like. Be consistent in capitalization.)

FIGURE 6.3a

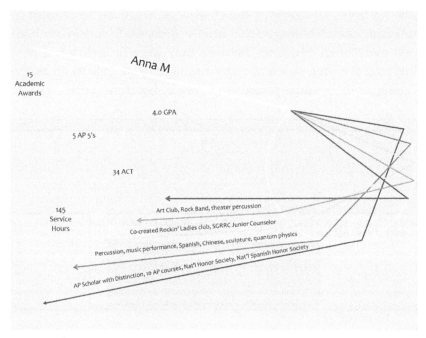

Anna M

15
Academic
Awards

4.0 GPA

5 AP 5's

34 ACT

145
Service
Hours

Art Club, Rock Band, theater percussion

Co-created Rockin' Ladies club, SGRRC Junior Counselor

Percussion, music performance, Spanish, Chinese, sculpture, quantum physics

AP Scholar with Distinction, 10 AP courses, Nat'l Honor Society, Nat'l Spanish Honor Society

FIGURE 6.3b

Anna's resume design actually came from her flipping through her physics textbook and seeing a graph that could serve as a template she could use while tinkering with her resume in ELA. Not all of the creative designs worked at first; they were too cluttered or the colors didn't quite mesh. But it was important to take a risk, ask what if, and tinker toward a new idea without the fear of getting it wrong. In the end, students are left with both resume versions, should they need both in the real world or college or the workforce. However, some students chose to fuse the best elements of both designs to create a new hybrid prototype that straddled the lines of *what is* and *what could be* (Figure 6.4).

Allowing for more tinkering and dabbling leads to more connections across disciplines and domains—in this case business, ELA, and graphic design. Sometimes, but not often, these interdisciplinary connections cause a fusion of ideas or combinations we haven't quite seen before. This is the Big-C Creativity mentioned several times already. For the classroom, we want to encourage tinkering and dabbling so that little-c moments of fusion can happen more often. Students, because they were tinkering and prototyping within a risk-ready environment, were able to break the ceiling of the resume project and create signature works.

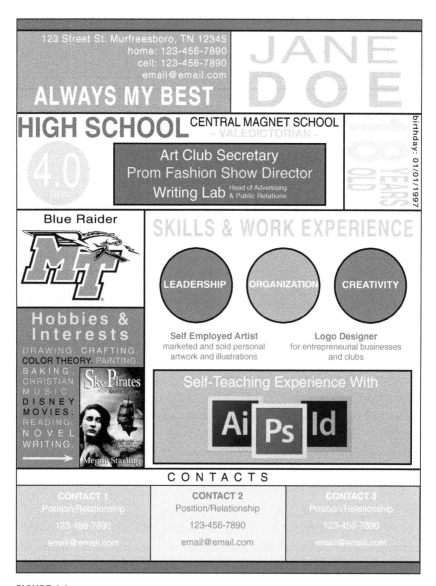

FIGURE 6.4a

FIGURE 6.4b

In addition to students laying multiple models side-by-side for the same project, we want students working on multiple projects at once as well. We want students working on various projects concurrently in order to provide incubation and reflection but also chances for cross-pollination. As Sawyer notes,

> Having more than one project under way means that if you reach an impasse on one project, you can just shift gears and move on to another project for a while, then

come back later. And it turns out that some of the best
ideas come from combining ideas across multiple projects.[8]

We absolutely agree, and an accidental fusion of projects occurred
at Lando's school that helped crystalize how creative projects
cannot be left to chance; they must be searched for, scouted,
and implemented within and beyond singular classroom walls.
In Lando's ELA class, students were freewriting one day and
were suddenly tasked to write a poem from the perspective of
a random color. With students used to the basket activity, they
immediately grabbed a slip and started writing from the perspective of blue, gold, orange, pink, and so on. Surprisingly, Lando
discovered that the art teacher down the hall was working on
a similar project where students would hone in on a specific
color and paint from that vantage point. Once this connection
was discovered, a *what if* from the teachers emerged: what if
we sent the color poems down to the art room to have the art
students visualize the poems and then display them side-by-
side in the hallway for the students to see while transitioning
to classes. The results were outstanding and completely unique
and unpredictable. The hallway display actually caused quite
the traffic jam during the initial days because the gallery was
set up without advertisement or notice; it just appeared one day.
This cross-pollination project between ELA and art became a
perennial favorite just like the resume project. With both teachers
and students operating as tinkerers and actively searching for
odd combinations and connections within and across discipline,
signature thinking can now happen *by design* for more students
more often.

Remember—It Starts with Us

When is the last time students did a project twice or—in the cases
above—three times in our classes? That's the engagement and drive
that is native to the creative classroom. This is also the reminder
that students need time to not only learn something deeply but

also to leverage the many tries needed to demonstrate that learning in a novel and signature way. Even with the aspirations of a risk-ready environment in place, we must remind ourselves that the power of tinkering and prototyping starts with us.

Starting with us means that we must model the process ourselves so that students see our own failed attempts and near-miss prototypes, whether that be the many essay drafts we are writing alongside students on *To Kill a Mockingbird* or multiple blueprints for a beach house. Show them your journal of what ifs or get in the R and D lab with students. Fully disclosing our tinkering process and our prototypes is crucial for convincing students to do the same and for adopting a tinkering mindset. The many iterations of this book and framework for creativity is a great example. We tinkered with the idea for signature thinking for years, and many of our breakthroughs came from creating, reflecting, and fusing ideas and prototypes (Figure 6.5).

FIGURE 6.5a

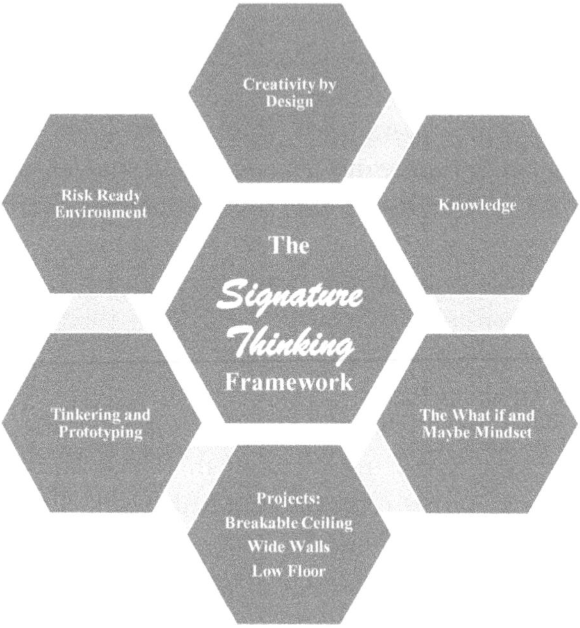

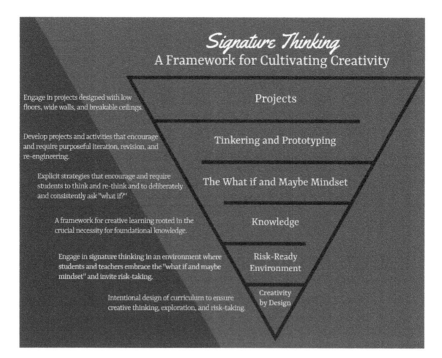

FIGURE 6.5b

FIGURE 6.5c

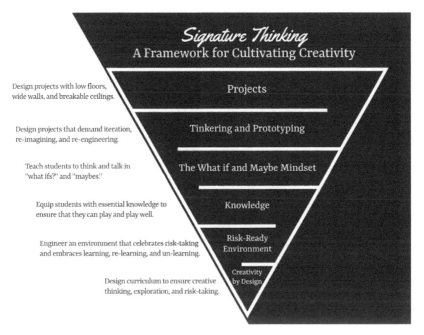

FIGURE 6.5d

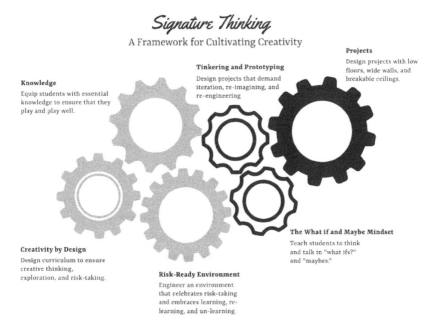

FIGURE 6.5e

Signature Thinking
The Key to Classroom Creativity

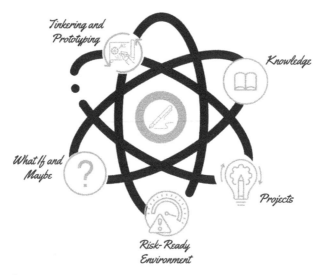

FIGURE 6.5f

We tinkered alongside our students as they created lesson plans, wrote book chapters, or even conducted dissertation research and experiments. It is imperative that students see us zig and zag across projects, and even more important that we consistently solicited feedback from our students' for how we can learn, grow, and break through. Making signature thinking work beyond a concept in our heads has been maddening, and we wouldn't have succeeded without help from our students.

The tinkering and prototyping process, when done openly and consistently from the teacher side, creates a sense of dual-risk taking where both teacher and student can learn reciprocally from each other. This powerful and vulnerable relationship is achieved, according to Resnick in *Lifelong Kindergarten*, when teachers are able to "move fluidly among the roles of catalyst, consultant, connector, and collaborator."[9] The benefits of this type of relationship for any learning, not just creative learning, cannot be overlooked and harkens back to the heart of a risk-ready environment: we all learn, innovate, and create by leaning into the unknown together.

Next, we must invite students to become co-designers in the creative curriculum we present. A great example of this comes from a project called *The Album Review* in Lando's ELA class. The first iteration of the project tasked students to select an album of their choice to listen to intently and then write a review in the style of *Rolling Stone, Pitchfork,* or *Consequence of Sound.* They were also forced to find other reviews to compare and contrast with their own arguments and claims. The students were excited and empowered and the project was a success. The next year, students began asking if they could add a design element to the written review so that it would look like a real review in *Rolling Stone.* Lando was nervous because he didn't know how to do that himself, but he greenlit the pivot to his original project and the results were exceptional.

In the next iteration the next year, students saw the current magazine style reviews and wanted to add a speaking and listening component to the project where they would defend their review in front of their peers while also providing targeted samplings of the actual music as well. Once more, the project shifted and changed into an even more creative endeavor than the teacher could have dreamed, all while collecting evidence of learning from a swath of state standards for ELA (Figure 6.6).

Students were invited to break, reshape, and break the project again each year. Essentially, the risk-ready environment helped the teacher move from *How dare you* to *I dare you* and relinquish control while widening the walls of what the project could be. The signatures that emerged were novel indeed.

In the end, we want our students to not only participate in the tinkering and prototyping process but to don the label with pride. *We are tinkerers in this class. We are tinkerers in this school.* For those worried about real-world skills, the persistence and perseverance seen in real life tinkerers is as real as it gets. Poet Marcus Jackson has admitted that some of his poems—some only a handful of lines—took him years to perfect. On a classroom scale, we see some students following in the same footsteps (Figures 6.7–6.10).

The Heart of Life ✗
We Are All Connected ✗ ⟶ Common Core

The Heart of Life

My favorite songwriter/poet of all time, John Mayer, wrote in a song: "No, it won't all go the way it should. But I know the Heart of Life is good." Standing in the presence of Almighty God in my church youth group, I finally realized this concept. Some people never realize it. We live in a very skeptic world, where we are either consciously or unconsciously taught by our elders that people are crazy and cannot be trusted. We are fed with stories and videos through media of people all over the world doing very bad things. This slowly turns us into skeptics of the human soul; callousing our hearts towards people simply because we can't seem to understand their actions. In my moment of epiphany during high school worship service, God revealed to me that people, in fact, are good. Ever since that night, I have been trying my best to challenge this common belief that the world is a bad place.

I am perpetually fascinated by how alike we all are. We try to pigeonhole people into different cliques or stereotypes or classes. Even from a young age, this is indeed our natural instinct. However, I don't believe that this is because we are evil. This is simply because we all have the common desire to fit in. To feel like we belong somewhere. This common thread of wanting to be liked and wishing to find our place in this world is actually what knits us all together. There is nothing evil about this, however I believe we all just go about it the wrong way.

On a daily basis, I try to challenge the idea of cliques at my High School. I don't just hang out with one group of friends, but many. I have even brought very different groups of people together. I learned long ago that you cannot judge people based on their actions, because you have no idea what they've been through that causes them to act the way they do. Even if people seem like they have bad intentions or make poor choices, I like to think that they simply just don't know how to respond to these situations in their lives. I believe that everyone is good in some way; we all simply disagree on how we show that goodness.

We have much more in common emotionally with other people than we think. Have you ever listened to a song and thought, "This perfectly describes my emotions/what I am going through"? I

speaks from music

FIGURE 6.6

Connected Through Music

One of my favorite song lyrics, written by Hunter Hayes, is: "It'll take some time, but I know that I can find where I belong, and I'll find it In a Song." His expression for finding comfort in the song lyrics of other artists caused me to realize that I'm not the only one who does this. The best feeling in the entire world is hearing a song that perfectly describes your emotions or the situations you are in. Why? I believe this is because we feel comforted by the fact that we are not the only ones who have felt a certain way; because someone, somewhere out there does, and cared enough to write a song about it. I believe that we are all far more connected than we think we are, and music helps us realize this.

Three years ago, I met someone who is now my best friend; and it all started with a song. I was with a large group of people, and one of my favorite songs, "The Great Escape" by Boys Like Girls, started playing. I was not the only one excited by this, but so was a girl in the group named Abby. We started talking about our connection with the angst-filled lyrics of wanting to leave our hometown and start over again. We realized that we had something in common; and a simple song written from the heart of a punk-pop lead singer helped us realize that.

Many people believe that we are all far too different from one another to ever get along. This bond that was formed with Abby from song lyrics made me pose the question of, "Are we really all that different?" Don't we all share the same common emotions; such as love, jealously, anger, impatience, and angst, with each other? If you break each song down by emotion, don't we all feel similar emotions?

For example, how could John Mayer write a song about a severed relationship that seems almost identical to the situation of my own broken heart? How could I possibly have anything in common, emotionally or circumstantially, with a 36 year old man from Connecticut? This cannot be a coincidence, but a thread from the common core of emotions and situations that knits us all together.

I began to challenge this idea that we are all too different to get along by befriending many different groups of people; people I formerly thought I could have nothing in common with. The

FIGURE 6.7

Connected Through Music

One of my favorite song lyrics, written by Hunter Hayes, is: "It'll take some time, but I know that I can find where I belong, and I'll find it In a Song." His expression for finding comfort in the song lyrics of other artists ~~caused me to realize~~ *brought me to the realization* that I'm not the only one who does this. The most wonderful feeling is hearing a song that perfectly describes your emotions or the situations you are in. Why? I believe this is because we feel comforted by the fact that we are not the only ones who have felt a certain way; because someone, somewhere out there does, and cared enough to write a song about it. I believe that we are all far more connected than we think we are, and music helps us realize this.

Three years ago, I met someone who is now my best friend; and it all started with a song. I was with a large group of people, and one of my favorite songs, "The Great Escape" by Boys Like Girls, started playing. I was not the only one excited by this, but so was a girl in the group named Abby. We started discussing our connection with the angst-filled lyrics of wanting to escape our hometown and start over again. We realized that we had something in common; and a simple song written from the heart of a Punk musician helped us realize that. This bond *formed* ~~that was formed~~ with a complete stranger, ~~simply~~ from song lyrics, made me pose the question of, "Are we really all that different?" Don't we all share the same common emotions; such as love, jealously, anger, impatience, and angst, with each other?

For example, how could John Mayer write a song about a severed relationship that seems almost *Echo?* identical to the situation of my own broken heart? How could I possibly have anything in common, emotionally or circumstantially, with a 36 year old man from Connecticut? This cannot be a coincidence, but a thread from the common core of emotions and situations that knits us all together. *In pursuit of these answers,* I began to challenge this idea that we are all too different to get along by befriending many different groups of people; people I formerly thought I could have nothing in common with. I found that though we may hold different beliefs or live our lives differently, our differing decisions all stem from very similar emotions. It is only how we go about dealing with these emotions that is different. *Good*

FIGURE 6.8

Connected Through Music

One of my favorite song lyrics, written by Hunter Hayes, is: "It'll take some time, but I know that I can find where I belong, and I'll find it In a Song." His expression for finding comfort in the song lyrics of other artists brought me to the realization that I'm not the only one who does this. The most magnificent feeling is hearing a song that perfectly describes your emotions or circumstances. Why? I believe this is because we feel comforted by the fact that we are not the only ones who have felt a certain way; because someone, somewhere out there does, and cared enough to write a song about it. I believe that we are all far more connected than we think we are, and music helps us realize this.

Three years ago, I met someone who is now my closest friend and it all began with a song. I was with a large group of people, and one of my favorite songs, "The Great Escape" by Boys Like Girls, started playing. I was not the only one excited by this, but so was a girl in the group named Abby. We began discussing our connection with the angst-filled lyrics of wanting to escape our hometown and start over again. We realized that we had something in common; and a simple song written from the heart of a Punk musician helped us realize that. This bond with a complete stranger, formed from song lyrics, made me pose the question of, "Are we really all that different?" Don't we all share the same common emotions; such as love, jealously, anger, impatience, and angst, with each other?

In pursuit of these answers, I began to challenge this idea that we are all too diverse or disconnected to get along by befriending many different groups of people; people I formerly thought I could have nothing in common with. I found that though we may hold contrasting beliefs or have various ways of living, our differing decisions all stem from very similar emotions. It is only how we go about dealing with these emotions that is different.

For example, how could John Mayer write a song about a severed relationship that echoes my own broken heart? How could I possibly have anything in common, emotionally or circumstantially, with a 36 year old man from Connecticut? This cannot be a coincidence but a thread from the common core of emotions that knits us all together.

FIGURE 6.9

Connected Through Music

One of my favorite song lyrics, written by Hunter Hayes, is: "It'll take some time, but I know that I can find where I belong, and I'll find it In a Song." His expression for finding comfort in the song lyrics of other artists brought me to the realization that I'm not the only one who does this. The most magnificent feeling is hearing a song that perfectly reflects your emotions or circumstances. Why? I believe this is because we are comforted knowing that we are not the only ones who have felt a certain way; because someone, somewhere out there does, and cared enough to write a song about it. I believe that we are all far more connected than we think we are, and music helps us realize this.

Three years ago, I met someone who is now my closest friend, and it all began with a song. I was with a large group of people, and one of my favorite songs, "The Great Escape" by Boys Like Girls, started playing. I was not the only one excited by this, but so was a girl in the group named Abby. We began discussing our connection with the angst-filled lyrics of wanting to escape our hometown and start over again. We realized that we had something in common; and a simple song written from the heart of a Punk musician helped us understand that. We found that although we have dissimilar interests and conflicting viewpoints on most topics, we both react to circumstances in almost an identical manner. This bond formed with a complete stranger, simply from song lyrics, made me pose the question of, "Are we really all that different?" Don't we all share the same common emotions; such as love, jealously, anger, impatience, and angst, with each other?

In pursuit of these answers, I began to challenge this idea that we are all too diverse or disconnected to get along. I did this by befriending many different groups of people; people I formerly thought I could have nothing in common with. I found that though we may hold contrasting beliefs or have various ways of living, our differing decisions all stem from very similar emotions. It is only how we go about dealing with these emotions that is different.

For example, how could John Mayer write a song about a severed relationship that echoes my own broken heart? How could I possibly have anything in common, emotionally or circumstantially,

FIGURE 6.10

Conclusion

We want tinkering to become the norm and yet we must ask ourselves: How often do our assignments and projects require students to revise, revisit, and re-engineer their ideas, their thinking, their products and designs? The tinkerer understands that quality and novel breakthroughs take time and tremendous effort. However, it will also take some convincing on the teacher side, but Suzie Boss reminds us that even with no time we must make time:

> Allow time in the project calendar for them to produce multiple drafts or prototypes. This is the *secret sauce* of PBL, leading to high-quality final work that students will be eager to present publicly.
>
> (p. 58)

And as Beghetto warns, it will also take time to convince students to think and act in these ways—to do the work twice or three times to get the best iteration. But the benefits of having students see creativity as an important part of their identity is worth the effort of establishing due date windows and not merely allowing students to try again but creating a culture where we demand it.[10]

Notes

1   Beghetto, *Beautiful Risks*, p. 64
2   Resnick, *Lifelong Kindergarten*, p. 136
3   Sawyer, *Zig Zag*, p. 173
4   Epstein, *Range*, p. 145
5   Resnick, *Lifelong Kindergarten*, p. 70
6   Sawyer, *Zig Zag*, p. master of choosing phrase
7   Seelig, *Ingenious*, p. 34
8   Sawyer, *Zig Zag*, p. 163
9   Resnick, *Lifelong Kindergarten*, p. 112
10 Beghetto, *Beautiful Risks* p. 64

7

Scaling Signature Thinking School-wide

Taking any new initiative to scale—whether it be curricular or pedagogical or both—is a challenge for all stakeholders involved. The new ways of thinking, the new materials, the new time constraints. All of these unknowns and more can cause anxiety about even the most exciting changes at a school. The ultimate aim of *signature thinking* is to help teachers and school leaders breach beyond the classroom level to establish a viable creative ecosystem that will help more students uncover their signatures more often. In essence, we want signature thinking to permeate the entire school culture. Unfortunately, schools won't become the creative havens of Renaissance Florence or Silicon Valley overnight. It will also be hard work. Resnick reminds us that most "scientists, inventors, and artists recognize that creativity is a long-term process."[1] So too for transforming a school into a creative hothouse. The following steps, however, provide the pathway to school-wide *signature thinking*.

DOI: 10.4324/9781003201380-7

ST Isn't Just Another Initiative

Initiative overload is a long and tiresome tradition in K12 education. In the case of creative curriculum, simply telling students to "be creative with it!" isn't enough. And yet, teachers have never been asked to juggle more than now, and a new curriculum asking for projects and tinkering can be overwhelming, especially if the curricular approach is unsound. Agarwal and Bain's *Powerful Teaching* is an excellent tour through some of the most sound science on how learning happens and yet also provides fair warnings against our longstanding habit to run with the next new thing in educational settings:

> We must stop driving instruction with anecdotes and fads, we must stop reinventing the wheel...Instead it's our responsibility to *ask for evidence*. Evidence for which strategies are effective, not just which strategies are popular.[2]

We couldn't agree more. However, we are fighting against decades of fads and misconceptions about creativity both in general and within classroom contexts. While we fall prey to the many myths of creativity—such as the *creative type* myth—we are also combating classroom mistruths about creativity. Ornamental creativity[3] is one of our biggest enemies. Kettler, Lamb, and Mullet provide this example:

> In some cases, teachers may hold myth-inspired views that are reflective of an ornamental view of creativity, as opposed to a cognitive view of creativity. For example, imagine a social studies project on the decline of the Roman Empire. Students individually conduct research on focused elements of the decline and synthesize those ideas into a brief paper and a display board. The teacher develops a rubric to help the students understand the assessment components of the project. In addition to the elements of the paper and the elements of the display, the teacher includes in the rubric 10 possible points

for creativity. When students ask for clarification, she describes creativity as use of color, borders, and illustrations as part of the display.[4]

This ornamental or decorative approach to creative thinking is not only unhelpful to productive creativity but, more importantly, also a waste of precious classroom time. Daniel Willingham[5] asks teachers to pause when designing learning experiences and ask: What will students be thinking about during this lesson, task, or project? In too many cases, students are thinking about an arts and crafts add-on instead of the content under study. We need to avoid sacrificing precious time in class to anything that draws student thinking away from our learning aims, and ornamental creative tasks too often do just that.

Similarly, Wiggins and McTighe warn against *hands-on, minds-off* learning where students create crafty add-ons to a project or dress up in costumes or decorate the room. Alternatively, real creative work demands discipline, persistence, and perseverance. It is full of *hard fun* and *serious play*. It demands, as we know from Chapter 3, both a depth and breadth of domain-specific knowledge. Signature Thinking is rooted in these truths and in the truths about how learning happens as well. Below, we outline how signature thinking feeds the science of learning:

◆ To be creative, students must *know* a great deal about the topic under study, and novel connections are often made with a complementary breadth of knowledge as well.
◆ Talking in what-ifs and maybes allows for idea exploration, tentative guesses, and helps feed a problem-finding habit.
◆ Project-based learning has many pitfalls, but by building a low-floor that guarantees bedrock knowledge is established, students can explore the helpful constraints of the project's wide walls and hopefully break the ceiling with their innovation.
◆ Spacing out learning and practice, as we have seen with S-PBL, helps ensure the *durability of learning*; cramming is largely ineffective for long-term retention.

♦ Learning is often non-linear and takes tons of time and many tries; tinkering and prototyping allows for all three.

♦ Incubation—time away from a problem or project—is crucial for making connections and generating break-through ideas.

♦ Creative thinking *is* critical thinking.

Creativity, therefore, shouldn't be a curricular add-on but a central feature—when implemented correctly. Helping students uncover and then hone their signatures has many benefits, from the economic pressures to innovate in the real world to the personal joy creativity brings. With signature thinking, we aim to reclaim creativity from the bin of educational clichés.

The Creative Teacher and the Creative Leader

The research isn't clear on exactly what makes a creative person, and pop culture myths make this even more muddied. But there is a trait that comes up perennially in the research across time and study types: *openness*. The willingness to step into the unknown and ask *what if* is a key signature of a creative thinker. Thus, we need an ecosystem that inculcates openness at every turn—in our activities and projects, in our rubrics and grade books, in our school-wide mission and vision, and in our teachers and school leaders themselves. Giving license, beyond the classroom level, to messiness, experimentation, risk-taking, innovation, questioning, collaboration, and tinkering encourages openness and helps the whole school get comfortable with uncertainty.

Beau Lotto's TED talk with his student Amy O'Toole contains a powerful call to action: "Step into uncertainty through the process of play."[6] His classroom motto, reminiscent of both Robinson and Resnick's philosophies, welcomes uncertainty and ambiguity. Beghetto, in his book *What if?*, echoes this sentiment as well: "Providing students with opportunities to learn how to respond productively to uncertainly will help prepare them for the kinds of real-world challenges they face now and will face in the future."[7] By leaning into the unknown in a risk-ready environment, we can get comfortable with not knowing and stumbling in the dark. We, just like our students, can make uncertainty our ally.

This is how humans grow new muscles, and teachers and school leaders must be ready to take this journey toward new thinking and new teaching themselves. *Signature Thinking* does demand a new type of teaching, which Sawyer calls *guided improvisation*.[8] Like a jazz musician, the creative teacher can shift and move with both the current classroom rhythms *and* capitalize on the detours and distractions. They are also skilled at *lesson unplanning*,[9] as Beghetto calls it, where existing plans and routines can be altered by inserting purposeful unknowns. The creative teacher can also build projects out of headlines at a moment's notice to harness the real-time issues of their communities and needs of their students.

One of the best ways to create more creative teachers is to embrace a culture of piloting within the school. The teaching staff must have license to tinker and dabble with small-scale pivots to instruction and assessment in order to make signature thinking happen school-wide. What if ELA, math, and art teachers could team up to create a STEAM project? What if science and social studies teachers could collaborate to tell the hard won story of a scientific breakthrough? With teachers themselves now asking what if and maybe, we need wide walls of our own to stay focused. Thus, school leaders must set the tone for creative thinking and teaching and provide the space for teachers to become tinkerers as well as *problem finders*—just like they are for their own students. Leaders can help teachers start small and avoid falling prey to *hands-on, minds-off* pitfalls by following a simple three-step process found in Jim Collins' *Great by Choice*.[10] When teachers want to dabble and get creative, ensure that their ideas meet these three criteria:

1. Is it low cost?
2. Is it low risk?
3. Is it low distraction?

According to Robinson, "the goal of a creative leader is not to have all the ideas; it is to encourage a culture where everyone has them."[11] If school leaders can check the three boxes above, through a short chat or a brief outline from the teacher, they can greenlight these what-ifs and maybes without sacrificing precious time for learning. Instead, sound, challenging, and engaging ideas and projects can permeate the school culture. However, even with the footing for implementing signature thinking outlined here, teachers and school leaders deserve the ongoing time and training and support it takes to become these jazz players. Sawyer illustrates key habits of mind championed by creative school leaders:

♦ School leaders shout, "We are a creative school!" They say it frequently, loudly, and publicly.
♦ School leaders give teachers professional development opportunities that focus on innovative teaching and learning.
♦ School leaders put systems in place that consistently recognize and reward creative teaching.
♦ School leaders welcome suggestions on how to make the school more conducive to creative teaching and learning.
♦ School leaders realize that teachers need to continually experiment in the class, and that this will lead teachers to occasionally make mistakes and encounter dead ends. School leaders are supportive when this happens.[12]

With teachers living out the strategies and mindsets outlined in the previous chapters, supported fully by their school leaders, *signature thinking* won't become just another initiative. It is about establishing a culture and recognizing that we have a calling as educators to not merely stand by and let creativity happen by chance. Instead, it begins with a recognition that we are called to establish a culture that promotes creativity for learning to help students grow in a way that is uniquely human. But there is also a consideration of the curriculum and *ST* should go deeper and broader than in one subject area.

ST Cuts Across All Disciplines

The research on teaching creativity points to the benefits of domain specificity. In other words, creativity in ELA looks different from math or science. According to Sawyer,

> Creativity tends to be specific to a domain—a discipline, subject, or field. That's why educating for creativity is more effective when it's integrated into every school subject, compared to teaching creativity as a general set of skills.[13]

The novelty of signature thinking, however, is its *crosscutting* features. Kettler, Lamb, and Mullet note that creativity in mathematics hinges upon asking good questions, "breaking from established mindsets," and considering and evaluating unusual mathematical ideas."[14] Further, in the sciences, students use their "existing knowledge of science to imagine a variety of solutions to problems."[15] These same traits can also be found in ELA and social studies classrooms where students ask provocative questions, explore ambiguous and unusual ideas, and dream up solutions to a range of problems. Signature thinking, once again, promotes asking what if and talking in maybes, which is beneficial no matter the discipline or domain. So too for tinkering and prototyping and multiple modeling. This crosswalk also helps combat the *creative type* myth where students often feel that because they aren't "artsy" that they aren't creative. Remember, we can all be creative—no matter the subject under study. Below are crosscutting habits of mind that thread through all the chapters of signature thinking:

- The ability for students to keenly see *what is* but also forecast *what could be* instead.
- The hunger for finding problems and seeking out solutions.
- The willingness to imagine multiple scenarios, outcomes, possibilities, and models.

- ◆ The persistence needed to vault over errors and impasses.
- ◆ The ability to fuse ideas, products, or innovations in novel combinations that work.

Domain specificity is undoubtedly crucial, but there is also room for fusion *within* and *across* domains. Thus, fidelity of implementation for signature thinking is eased because of the zig zag nature of its crosscutting features, making launching and sustaining these features customizable and feasible. Clark and Jain discuss this with regards to the curriculum:

> the trunk of the curriculum cannot exist in isolation. A healthy culture must provide the soil to nourish the tree, and… the sun causes the trunk to extend heavenward with new branches in fruit. When all three of these elements: curriculum, culture, and calling, are in place, the school grows and thrives. When one or the other of these things is weakened, the school becomes sickly.[16]

Signature Thinking, taken to scale, equips "schools" with all the elements to maximize productive creativity and student learning. Essentially, Beghetto's advice rings true once again: teachers simply need to look for the creative openings in the curriculum and seize those opportunities for students to make their marks.

Expos, Showcases, and Events

The heart of a signature school is the many ways we showcase and celebrate creative work to all stakeholders, including students, teachers, school leaders, parents, and community members. We aim to do this all the time and in both domain-specific and interdisciplinary ways. One of the best examples of this in action is seen in the documentary *Most Likely to Succeed*,[17] a profile of High Tech High in San Diego where students are given wide-walled projects to complete and products and innovations are displayed and defended publicly. With R and D spaces placed in classrooms across the school, no matter the discipline, we are now equipped and ready to showcase students' signatures in a celebratory and public fashion as well.

The root of such events traces back to what started as an open mic poetry night at Lando's school. Students across the entire school were invited to submit poems to read to a real audience of peers, parents, and community members. The event was stocked with food and refreshments and wired for sound by a professional music shop in town. Most important, the event was free for all. This event was an immediate success, and students from all backgrounds made the courageous leap into the unknown to read original works of poetry. Over the years, the event grew into a poetry and art showcase. The final iteration added a miniature music concert. The event, after many years of tinkering and prototyping, became an all-inclusive showcase called *A Night at the Arts*. The open invitation to participate was an empowering opportunity to reinforce the truth that *all students* have a creative capacity.

However, at the same school events beyond the arts were important as well, which also combated the myth that creativity is bound to the arts alone. The Senior Thesis Expo was a public event where students such as the body armor team could reveal their final product to the community and local professionals in STEM fields. The day-long event allowed students to engage with scientists, engineers, and healthcare professionals from the local universities, firms, and hospitals. Student work was celebrated and also recalibrated based upon expert feedback so that students could continue the tinkering process before their final TED-like presentations before graduation.

Remember that the best and brightest aren't always the *rightest*; they experience tons of failure to get to where they are in a field or career. As Firestein reminds us, "Things don't happen in the linear or narrative way that you read about in papers or textbooks. The smooth 'Arc of Discovery' is a myth."[18] We want to honor that truth with an event that's a little bit different, an event that showcases failed prototypes and near-misses and celebrates failure school-wide. Modeled from the now defunct *Museum of Failure*,[19] which was an open warehouse of innovations that didn't quite work, we encourage hosting an event called the *Fail Fair* where students and teachers can celebrate successful creations side-by-side with near-misses. This interdisciplinary event provides chances for students and their own teachers to display a portfolio of work that is polished, in-progress, or even abandoned. This event can take place mid-year or as the culminating event of the school year. Regardless, the point is for students to openly share their zig-zag path toward something creative. For example, a student could share the messy journey of writing a book of short stories and include prototypes of the book cover, character sketches, conflict maps, and save time to read the dust jacket synopsis to audience members. Further, another student could tell the story of tinkering toward a new type of shopping cart buggy where a patent map shows the *what is* so that the student can showcase *would could be* with their innovation. Another student could display their debugging records along with the source code that finally worked for a new program or app. It is important to have *all students* show *all prototypes*—even the ugly ones—built along the way in the classroom setting and have them narrate their persistent and consistent drive through impasses and dead ends toward something novel that works. The final element is having teachers participate right alongside students at the *Fail Fair*. This is where teachers share their own what-ifs, tinkering processes, and prototypes. Share lesson plans that bombed, projects that were scrapped, and creative endeavors from beyond the school setting as well. Showcase a failed garden or a wrecked home renovation. It is imperative that students see their teachers take risks and understand that not every endeavor pans out. According to Hope and Wade King, authors of *The Wild Card*, "children need to learn that no one can succeed at every attempt and that it's important to keep working."[20] Remember, as we have said throughout the book, it starts with us.

Conclusion

The journey toward a signature school is a zig-zag in of itself. Renaissance Florence and Silicon Valley were creative hubs built *by design* through intentional architectural and structural openness that provided chances for diverse people and divergent ideas to collide. How can we tinker with the campus map or master schedule to ensure this happens for students in a similarly intentional way? When we scale *ST* school-wide, we bust the myth that creativity is just for the arts or for a specific niche of students. Instead, we not only empower all students to uncover and sharpen their signatures but we also equip them with the tools to do so within and beyond the school day. By using the strategies and mindsets presented in this book, more students can discover how to put their twist, take, spin, or mark on their work. They will be ready and willing to do something *a little bit different* and enjoy the full fruits of their creative capacity. They will become *signature thinkers*.

Notes

1   Resnick, *Lifelong Kindergarten*, p. 20
2   Agarwal & Bain, *Powerful Teaching*, p. 7
3   Kettner, Lamb, & Mullet, *Developing Creativity in the Classroom*, p. 21
4   Kettner, Lamb, & Mullet, *Developing Creativity in the Classroom*, p. 22
5   Willingham, *Why Student's Don't Like School*
6   Beau Lotto, "Science is for Everyone," TED Talk, 2014.
7   Beghetto, *What If?*, p. 2
8   Sawyer, *Creative Schools*, p. 35
9   Beghetto, *What If*, p. 43
10 Collins and Hansen, *Great by Choice*, p. 81
11 Robinson, *Creative Schools*, p. 205
12 Sawyer, *The Creative Classroom*, p. 85
13 Sawyer, *The Creative Classroom*, p. 32
14 Kettner, Lamb, & Mullet, *Developing Creativity in the Classroom*, p. 24

15 Kettner, Lamb, & Mullet, *Developing Creativity in the Classroom*, p. 25
16 Clark and Jain, *The Liberal Arts Tradition*, p. 144
17 This documentary, inspired by Wagner's book of the same title, can be downloaded via iTunes.
18 Firestein, *Failure*, p. 92
19 Although the Museum of Failure is no more, this website allows students to tour the museum virtually: https://museumoffailure.com/
20 King & King, *The Wild Card*, p. 117

References

Agarwal, P. K. & Bain, P. M. (2019). *Powerful teaching: Unleash the science of learning.* San Francisco, CA: Jossey-Bass.

Amabile, T. (2012). *Big C, little C, Howard, and me: Approaches to understanding creativity.* Working paper, Harvard Business School, September 30, 2012. Available online at: <https://www.hbs.edu/ris/Publication%20Files/12-085_eb9ecda0-ec0a-4a32-8747-884303f8b4dd.pdf >

Bartsch, L. M. & Oberauer, K. (2021). The effects of elaboration on working memory and long-term memory across age. *Journal of memory and language,* 118: 104215.

Beevor, L. & Green, S. (2018). *Amazing women: 101 lives to inspire you.* Tulsa, OK: Stripes Publishing.

Beghetto, R. (2018). *Beautiful risks: Having the courage to teach and learn creatively.* Lanham, MD: Rowman and Littlefield.

Beghetto, R. (2016). Respond creatively: A small-steps approach. In *Big wins, small steps* (pp. 1–12). Corwin. https://www.doi.org/10.4135/9781506343020.n1

Beghetto, R. (2018). *What If? Building students' problem-solving skills through complex challenges.* Alexandria, VA: ASCD.

Boss, S. (2015). *Implementing project-based learning.* Bloomington, IN: Solution Tree.

Brown, P. C., Roediger, H. L., & McDaniel, M. A. (2014). *Make it stick: The science of successful learning.* Cambridge, MA: Belknap Press of Harvard University Press.

Burkus, D. (2014). *The myths of creativity: The truth about how innovative companies and people generate great ideas.* San Francisco, CA: Jossey-Bass.

Clark, K. & Jain, R. S. (2013). *The liberal arts tradition: A philosophy of Christian classical education.* Camp Hill, PA: Classical Academic Press.

Clinton, C. & Boiger, A. (2017). *She persisted: 13 American women who changed the world*. New York, NY: Philomel Books.

Collins, J. & Hansen, M. T. (2011). *Great by choice: Uncertainty, chaos, and luck – why some thrive despite them all*. New York, NY: HarperCollins.

Couros, G. (2015). *The innovator's mindset: Empower learning, unleash talent, and lead a culture of creativity*. San Diego, CA: Dave Burgess Consulting, Inc.

Craik, F. I. M. & Tulving, E. (1975). Depth of processing and the retention of words in episodic memory. *Journal of experimental psychology,* 104(3): 268–294.

Cronin, M. A. & Loewenstein, J. (2013). *The craft of creativity*. Stanford, CA: Stanford Business Books.

Csikszentmihalyi, M. (2013). *Creativity: Flow and the psychology of discovery and invention*. New York, NY: Harper Collins.

Epstein, D. (2019). *Range: Why generalists triumph in a specialized world*. New York, NY: Riverhead Books.

Firestein, S. (2015). *Failure: Why science is so successful*. New York, NY: Oxford University Press.

Hattie, J. (2012). *Visible learning for teachers: Maximizing impact on learning*. New York, NY: Routledge.

Karpicke, J. D., Blunt, J. R., Smith, M. A., & Karpicke, S. S. (2014). Retrieval-based learning: The need for guided retrieval in elementary school children. *Journal of applied research in memory and cognition,* 3: 198–206.

Kettler, T., Lamb, K. N., & Mullet, D. R. (2018). *Developing creativity in the classroom: Learning and innovation for 21st-century schools*. Waco, TX: Prufrock Press.

King, H. & King, W. (2018). *The wild card: 7 steps to an educator's creative breakthrough*. San Diego, CA: Dave Burgess Consulting, Inc.

Kunstler, B. (2013). *The hothouse effect: Intensify creativity in your organization using secrets from history's most innovative communities*. New York, NY: AMACOM.

Martin. R. (2019). "Kids' Author Mo Willems Has a New Creative Challenge (And So Should You)." *NPR.* July 2.

Pieper, J. (2009). *Leisure: The basis of culture*. San Francisco, CA: Ignatius Press.

Pink, D. H. (2011). *Drive: The surprising truth about what motivates us.* New York, NY: Riverhead Books.

Realtime. (2019, June 7). *Andrew Yang: Realtime with Bill Maher* [Video]. YouTube.

Resnick, M. (2018). *Lifelong kindergarten: Cultivating creativity through projects, passion, peers, and play.* Cambridge, MA: The MIT Press.

Robinson, K. & Aronica, L. (2016). *Creative schools: The grassroots revolution that's transforming education.* New York, NY: Penguin Books.

Sawyer, K. (2014). *Zig zag: The surprising path to greater creativity.* San Francisco, CA: Jossey-Bass.

Sawyer, K. (2019). *The creative classroom: Innovative teaching for 21st century learners.* New York, NY: Teachers College Press.

Seelig, T. (2015). *InGenius: A crash course on creativity.* New York, NY: HarperOne.

Seixas, P. & Morton, T. (2013). *The big six: Historical thinking concepts.* Nelson.

Stronge, J. (2018). *Qualities of effective teachers.* (3rd Ed.). Alexandria, VA: ASCD.

Wagner, T. (2014). *The global achievement gap: Whey our kids don't have the skills they need for college, careers, and citizenship – and what we can do about it.* New York, NY: Basic Books.

Wagner, T. (2015). *Creating innovators: The making of young people who will change the world.* New York, NY: Scribner.

Wiggins, G. & McTighe, J. (2005). *Understanding by design.* (2nd Ed.). Alexandria, VA: ASCD.

Willingham, D. T. (2009). *Why students don't like school? A cognitive scientist answers questions about the mind.* (1st Ed.). San Francisco, CA: Jossey-Bass.